Exploring Spirit

Exploring Spirit

Finding what matters in a broken world

Giles Goddard

© Giles Goddard 2026

First published in 2026 by the Canterbury Press Norwich

Editorial office
3rd Floor, Invicta House
110 Golden Lane,
London EC1Y 0TG, UK
www.canterburypress.co.uk

Canterbury Press is an imprint of Hymns Ancient & Modern Ltd
(a registered charity)

Hymns Ancient & Modern® is a registered trademark of
Hymns Ancient & Modern Ltd
13A Hellesdon Park Road, Norwich,
Norfolk NR6 5DR, UK

All rights reserved. No part of this publication may be reproduced,
stored in a retrieval system, or transmitted,
in any form or by any means, electronic, mechanical,
photocopying or otherwise, without the prior permission of
the publisher, Canterbury Press.

Giles Goddard has asserted his right under the Copyright, Designs and
Patents Act 1988 to be identified as the Author of this Work

Scripture quotations are from New Revised Standard Version
Bible: Anglicized Edition, copyright © 1989, 1995 National
Council of the Churches of Christ in the United States of America.
Used by permission. All rights reserved worldwide.

British Library Cataloguing in Publication data
A catalogue record for this book is available
from the British Library

ISBN: 978 1-78622-649-5

EU GPSR Authorised Representative
LOGOS EUROPE, 9 rue Nicolas Poussin, 17000, LA ROCHELLE, France
E-mail: Contact@logoseurope.eu

No part of this book may be used or reproduced in any manner for the
purpose of training artificial intelligence technologies or systems.

Typeset by Regent Typesetting

Contents

Part 1 Where on earth are we going?

1	I am doing a new thing	3
2	Where are we now?	15
3	How did we get here?	23

Part 2 How do we get there?

4	Exploring creation	31
5	Exploring bodies	38
6	Exploring nature	50
7	Exploring lament	59
8	Exploring death	70
9	Exploring justice	79
10	Exploring light	90

Part 3 Is there a 'there' there?

11	The maze of city streets	103
12	Mountains of the mind	110
13	God is a verb	117
14	Here I am!	127

Acknowledgements	135
Further reading	136
References	137

There is a tradition of the Prophet Mohammed, peace be upon him, in which God tells him: 'I am as My servant thinks (expects) I am. I am with them when they mention Me. If they mention Me to themselves, I mention them to Myself; and if they mention Me in an assembly, I mention them in an assembly greater than it. If they draw near to Me a hand's length, I draw near to them an arm's length. And if they come to Me walking, I go to them running.'

Hadith Qudsi, in Sahīh al-Bukhāri (121:9 #7405)

O Holy Power who forged the Way for us!
You penetrate all in heaven and earth and even down below.
You're everything in One.
Through You, clouds billow and roll and winds fly!
Seeds drip juice,
springs bubble into brooks, and
spring's refreshing greens flow – through You – over all
   the earth!
You also lead my spirit into Fullness.
Holy Power, blow wisdom in my soul and – with your
   wisdom – Joy!

> Carmen Acevedo Butcher, *Incandescence: 365 Readings with Women Mystics* (Paraclete Press, 2005), translating Hildegard of Bingen's Sequence O *ignis Spiritus paracliti* (O fire of the Spirit)

For the people of St John's, Waterloo

PART I

Where on earth are we going?

I

I am doing a new thing

'If you know Nigerians,' said Chine, 'we get married loudly, we christen loudly, and we die loudly. One of my strongest memories is of my husband and me at my grandmother's funeral, dancing up the aisle – celebrating the birth of our eldest son.'

We laughed as Chine went on to describe that moment of lament and joy. She spoke of the immense sadness she felt on the death of her grandmother, the grief that was unleashed at the funeral – and how this morphed into joy as, all unplanned, the assembled mourners turned to the future and welcomed her tiny child very recently arrived in this world.

Chine McDonald, director of the think tank Theos, was speaking as part of the season of talks we held at St John's, Waterloo, in 2024. Entitled Exploring Spirit, the season aimed to open up ideas about spirituality in its widest sense. It was the second season of Exploring Spirit events. The first, in 2023, had been well received as a series of talks and workshops, films celebrating the life of Martin Luther King to celebrate Black History Month, and a group focus on ecology and the earth in responding to the climate crisis – all aiming to offer food for the spirit.

In 2024 we ran the season again. Twenty or so people gathered on chairs and on beanbags under the historic brick vaulting of the crypt at St John's, engaging with speakers from around the world and across the spectrum of belief and practice.

The day after Chine's talk we received an email:

> I write about the Exploring the Spirit session I attended last night. When I turned up a bit late, Chine the speaker had already finished her talk and the breakout group discussions were underway.

I asked a vicar what exactly was being discussed, to which he responded saying it was to do with Black Lives Matter and the summer riots. As the evening wore on, it became abundantly clear that you were not discussing biblical truth and concepts at all, the 'spirit' with a lower case was about discussing how all faiths and other persuasions felt about joy and spirit (not sure where justice featured?) with someone sharing something about climate activism.

I wish to make a formal complaint that what you're advertising is extremely misleading and frankly heretical, and is absolutely not what I came for. I was horrified when, as we were leaving, the same vicar asked me whether I came from a Hindu background because a Hindu and a Muslim are coming to share about their spirituality in a church!!

I can't think of anything more pagan and heretical. When I must've expressed surprise, he patronizingly said, 'God is bigger than church'!

I'd like my travel costs re-imbursed totalling £16.80. I attach a screenshot of my credit card entry.

My heart sank. Not because of the complaint; as vicar of a church I have come to expect regular complaints, and they usually slide off me once I have decided how to respond and what, if anything, needs changing. My heart sank because the email showed a complete misunderstanding of what we were doing. We had advertised the season as

> An interfaith series of talks and discussion for anyone looking to explore faith, the spiritual and God. Exploring Spirit will encourage you to contemplate your own spiritual life and to explore the spirituality of the world through many different topics and spaces.
>
> This seven-week series will consist of talks and discussions giving a chance for us all to nurture our spiritual selves. Topics include: spirit and creativity, spirit and justice, spirit and death, spirit and beauty.

I AM DOING A NEW THING

Our complainant had clearly not absorbed what we said – but more than that, she had leapt on to the barricades as soon as she realized that what we were offering didn't fit her idea of what a church should do.

This book is not for her. It is for you if you are a person who is seeking a deeper understanding of what it means to be human, under the eye of some kind of glimpsingly understood divinity. It is for you if you want to draw water from the wells of wisdom provided by the generations of seekers who have gone before us. It is for you if you are perplexed and confused about how life can at the same time be beautiful and utterly tragic, or about how horrific wickedness and violence can coexist with astonishing beauty and selflessness. It is for you if you want to explore spirituality. It is not a book of answers. It is a palimpsest of thoughts and ideas that may, taken together, help you in your exploration. I hope so.

* * *

The idea for *Exploring Spirit* emerged from many conversations. With Henry, for example.[1]

'What brought you to St John's?' I asked him one Sunday morning soon after he arrived.

'It's a long story,' he said. 'In some ways. But not in others.'

'What does that mean?'

He looked away.

'Maybe I'll tell you, sometime. I'm here now, though, and glad I came.'

Around us was the hubbub of post-church chat. The usual queue for hot drinks, the smell of freshly brewed coffee, excitement over the cutting of a birthday cake for Susan. Henry was tentative, spoke quietly, had braved the coffee bear pit but stood not talking to anyone.

'Come again,' I said. He took a sip of his coffee and munched the last of his chocolate biscuit.

'I think I will. I enjoyed it. The worship wasn't familiar to me. But I'm not at all sure what I believe. Would that be a problem?'

I laughed.

'Not at all. We have a wide range of beliefs here, from agnostic – atheist, really – to very traditionally devout. You'd be one among many.'

'That's a relief,' he said. 'I may well be back. Thank you for the coffee, and the service.'

There's another, I thought as he left, cautiously seeking. He was in his mid-twenties, a chunky silver ring in his septum. He held my gaze as he spoke, but I picked up a reserve that led me to think we might have seen the last of him.

There were others. We have a steady flow, often people in their twenties and thirties, who find their way to St John's via the internet or social media or word of mouth. I, or one of my colleagues, usually fix a coffee with new arrivals so that we can talk properly. The coffees are accompanied by conversations that are rarely awkward and nearly always enriching. Sitting over a steaming turmeric latte in Caffè Nero on the Cut in south London, I ask why they have searched us out, and usually I receive a full and thoughtful response.

'I have a desire for something, but I'm not sure what,' said Francesca. 'I love this city, I love what I'm doing, I'm enjoying my Master's although it's hard and the teaching isn't as good as I had hoped. But I'm looking for something more. I can't put my finger on what that might be. It's not the religion I had as a child, that stern Catholicism in Italy, in Viterbo, my mother making me go to Mass every week. I hated it, and after a while I rebelled and refused. I could never go back to that. But there's something else I want to find, and maybe I can find it here.'

Deepti, drinking tee tarik, the closest she could find to Indian chai, in Roti King on Lower Marsh in south London, eating flatbread and jackfruit rendang. 'I stopped going to the temple as soon as I could. I didn't like the priests. It didn't feel right, what they did and how they spoke. But I missed the colour and the drama and all the craziness of it.'

'I'm not sure that we're very crazy,' I said.

'Maybe not,' she smiled, 'but you have a lot of ritual and I like the beauty of the place. It feels OK. No elephants, true, but hey, who needs elephants to worship?'

'When you have Jesus.'

'Well, that's what I'm trying to find out more about. Who is this Jesus and why do you worship him?'

'That's a big question which would take a while to answer,' I said.

'Try me.' She smiled and scooped up a mouthful of rendang.

Henry did come back, and had tea in the vicarage.

'My grandmother, she took me to church. My parents didn't believe, and it didn't mean much to me, but it was important to her and so my parents let it happen. I think they hoped that some of the 'Christian' virtues might rub off on me. Not sure they ever did, and I stopped going as I got older and was able to wriggle out of Grandma's expectations – with my parents' support. But I remembered the church, and now that I'm in London there's something about it which feels', he stopped, thought a bit, '... intriguing.'

There are common themes. Many of the people who find their way to St John's identify as LGBTI+ or queer. They come to us seeking a place where they can search in safety, where they can explore the connections between spirituality and identity without fear of condemnation, often escaping from places where they have not been welcome.

Many are seeking somewhere that resonates with childhood memories. They have a desire for something a bit theatrical, maybe, and something that reflects the sense of community they remember from when they were young. There is often a feeling of loss, of missing something, hard to define but there nonetheless. Perhaps, an emptiness. Above all, a desire to explore this notion of spirituality: what is it, how do I find it, what's it all about?

***

Before trying to answer that, I need to deal with the slippery question of language. What do we talk about when we talk about God? The difficulty with all religious language is that it can only be metaphorical. It is referring to things that are indescribable. God, heaven, hell, eternity, salvation ... all these words are pointing to things beyond human understanding, and we use words that can only sketch a meaning. God, heaven, hell, eternity, salvation – they are all beyond time and space, outside human perception.

The word 'god' has been used in what feels like an infinity of senses. God as nature, god in nature, god beyond nature, many gods in many guises, Greek gods making playthings of their human subjects, Hindu gods in dalliance in their temples, Norse gods with their tricksters and tyrants, Allah's self-disclosure in the Qur'an as fully intimate with the created order yet incomparable to creation, the back parts of God seen by Moses in the book of Exodus, the god of stones, the god of iron, god as vengeance, god as love ... what on earth is going on? In this book, when I use the word 'god' with a lower-case g, I am referring to a supreme being, the life force in its totality, the divine, infinite existence – or, occasionally, particular gods of polytheistic religions – Krishna, Odin, Huitzilopochtli. When I refer to God with a capital G I am referring to the Christian conception of God, the Trinity, the Creator, Redeemer and Sustainer. I use Allah to denote the Islamic conception of God, Yahweh the Jewish.[2]

But there is a strong tradition within theology which holds that there is nothing that can be said about God, because whatever we say is untrue – God's goodness is beyond our idea of goodness, God's eternity is beyond our idea of time. This strand of thinking about God and spirit is known as the apophatic tradition – *apo* is Greek for 'from' and *phatic* relates to speech. Many of the great mystics were part of the apophatic tradition – for example, the author of *The Cloud of Unknowing* – and we will be delving into their thought-worlds later.

There is, however, a contrary word that is also helpful – kataphatic – which brings us back to the possibility of talking about god and spirit. Kataphatic theology holds that the language we use does help us to understand spirituality better – if we say that god is good, or eternal, we can acknowledge that the words are inadequate but still use them as pointers towards that which can't be fully described.

If we are exploring spirituality, we have to be able to speak about god, but it's also important to recognize that whatever we say isn't really adequate – so we'll be using both traditions as we set out on the journey ahead. We'll pass through the kataphatic towards the apophatic, because both provide illumination (another metaphor!) about the spiritual path.

But that begs another question: what do we talk about when we talk about spirit? It's a word that has many meanings. One study, published in 2005, identified 27 distinct definitions, 'among which there was little agreement'.[3] The word comes from the Latin word *spiritus* meaning breath, breathing or a light wind. *Spiritus* is used in the earliest Latin translations of the Bible for the Hebrew word *ruach*, which also means breath or wind. *Ruach* is the word used at the beginning of Genesis:

> In the beginning when God created the heavens and the earth, the earth was a formless void and darkness covered the face of the deep, while a wind from God [*ruach/spiritus*] swept over the face of the waters.(Gen. 1.1–2)

Ruach has a close relation in Arabic – *ruh* – which occurs frequently in the Qur'an and also means breath or spirit. Paul, in his letters in the New Testament, often uses the Greek word *pneuma*, meaning breath, spirit or soul, also translated into Latin as *spiritus* to describe both the spirit within human beings and the Holy Spirit.

So spirit, as breath or air, is what gives life. To be inspired is, at its simplest, to be filled with breath. 'God formed man from the dust of the ground,' we read in Genesis, 'and breathed into his nostrils the breath of life' (Gen. 2.7). In classical philosophy, the spirit is the animator, the force that gives life to the body. The use of the term to describe alcoholic drinks is not coincidental. The process of distillation produces a clear liquid which early alchemists thought was the essence of the liquid being distilled, whether rosewater or fermented potatoes. That liquid was known in earlier centuries as aqua vitae, the water of life.

In more recent times spirituality is often placed in opposition to religion. 'I'm spiritual but not religious,' I hear people say, as if religion could not possibly be the spiritual – as if the two are mutually incompatible. 'I have a problem with organized religion. I get my spirituality from nature.'

It's true that places of worship are too often conservative and exclusionary. Their leaders, their congregations refuse to welcome women and lesbian, gay and trans people on equal terms. There is longstanding racism among white-majority churches, and the appalling history of child abuse has undermined any legacy of trust. So places of worship are often shunned by people seeking answers to fundamental questions.

That's a tragedy. Organized religion, shared worship, rituals of faith – they're all collective efforts to reach towards the transcendent and are expressions of the human yearning for the infinite. Church steeples in the heart of English villages, the domes of mosques symbolizing the cosmos – these are the places where, over centuries, people have come together with their questions and their doubts, their hopes and their fears, and have explored the life of the spirit. The ancient religious traditions are full of spiritual wisdom; they are the accumulations of centuries of reflecting, writing, thinking, praying, living and dying. Yes, there has been venality and corruption and abuse, but there have also been stories, sometimes painful and sometimes redemptive, and answers, sometimes conflicting and sometimes enlivening. Without them we would be less than the people we are created to be.

From earliest times, human beings have tried to make sense of a world that feels very big and often hostile. Some have sought to placate the gods through sacrifice and offerings, and tried to get the gods on their side through prayer. Others have come to believe that by allowing their inner spirit to flourish, they can be transformed. There is a dynamism in the spiritual life that speaks of the inflow and expiration of breath, of change and impermanence. It also speaks of a reality that is beyond our earth-bound ability to grasp fully, but through spiritual exercises and exploration we can begin to see through a glass, darkly, the deep reality that underpins the entire cosmos.

So the many meanings and uses of the word tell me that it is unwise to try to define it too tightly. In this book I propose to use 'spirit' to mean that part of human consciousness which reaches towards the infinite.

But this blurs a very significant boundary. If I am defining spirit in this way, am I not excluding spirit as agent – spirit as the force that draws us in, which is outside our consciousness but resonates with that deep part of ourselves that is searching for meaning?

It's not an either/or question. Spirit is both the breaking-in of the infinite into the world and the part of ourselves that seeks that infinite. So spirit (external) resonates with spirit (internal) in so far as we are trying to make sense of all those things beyond description and beyond the edge of the universe. It's like two violin strings vibrating in harmony with each other, making a sound beyond anything one string could make on its own.

Within Christian theology, there is also the Spirit – the third person of the Trinity, which, we are told in Acts, was given to the disciples after Jesus' resurrection, and which inspired them to create the church. I don't propose to delve into the theology of the Trinity in this book – there isn't time, and thousands of books have been written and gallons of blood spilled over precisely how the Trinity is understood. But when I capitalize Spirit I am referring specifically to that mode of the Trinitarian God.

I use the word soul rarely. In many spiritual traditions, the soul is the essence of a person, encompassing their thoughts, emotions, personality and beliefs, while the spirit is the immaterial part that connects with a higher power or the divine; essentially, the soul is who you are while the spirit is your connection to something greater than yourself. But the two words are often used interchangeably, which can be confusing. There is crossover between soul and spirit. At heart, both the soul and the spirit can denote that part of our consciousness which reaches towards the infinite. It is more straightforward to use one word, and so I will take spirit to include soul.

***

I am inviting you to join me on a journey which has been taken by millions of people over thousands of years, into the spaces between words and the gaps between galaxies. It's an exciting journey. Like anything rewarding, it needs work, time, commitment, practice. It's also a difficult journey. It involves setbacks and challenges. You may get lost. It may feel as though you are in a wilderness where there are no paths, or if there are paths it's not clear where they lead. I think of those tiny Voyager probes exploring the solar system, curving across the spaces between the planets and eventually leaving the solar system far behind, rushing through the void towards a billion other stars.

You are not alone. There are signs that can be read, and there are things around that can help you find your way. You will, I am certain, meet in the wilderness people who will offer to guide you. But by what authority do you trust the people you meet? Starting right here – what gives me the authority to write this book?

I long to share the journey because it has given me a far deeper understanding than I thought possible about who we are and why we exist. I have told the story in my book *Generous Faith* and will not repeat it in detail here. But an outline may explain why I think I have something worth sharing.

When I was ordained, in 1995, I was ambivalent at best about the idea of 'god'. I often used phrases such as 'whatever we mean by the word god' in my sermons, and avoided serious god-talk. I thought that the practice of worship was important – the coming together in church of very diverse groups of people who wanted to share a spiritual journey and were often passionate about working for a better world – but I was by no means sure what lay behind it.

I had a strong commitment to the justice that the Gospels call for and affection for the communities that gather around churches, but I had not begun to discover the unplumbable depths of the spiritual journey, the dark oceans into which we are invited to dive. I loved the Christian story, and loved the way we acted it out, collectively, year after year in the Christian calendar: Christmas, Lent, Easter, Pentecost – birth and death and resurrection. I was sure that Christianity was about love, inclusion and welcome. But it often felt, looking back, as if I was going through the motions.

Stories drew me in. The stories of people around me whose lives had been changed through their embrace of the spiritual. Frank, whose life fell apart when his wife left him and who was on the edge of taking his own life when he had a feeling of such love that he swore never to think about suicide again, and to follow the path of God wherever it led. Sheila, whose quiet determination to welcome the outsider and bring in people on the edge often landed her in trouble, but she was never daunted. People who derived their strength from a commitment to the thing I spoke about but rarely allowed into my head or heart.

Slowly, and with much help, I began to find that there really is more to life than appears on the surface. I read a book called *Original Blessing* by a great priest and monk, Matthew Fox, which challenged the prevalence of the doctrine of original sin in Western theology. My spiritual director, Julie Dunstan, helped me to bring together the very divergent parts of my life as a gay man in London and as a priest in the Church of England. She encouraged me to take up contemplative prayer, and to spend time in silence every day. I began to learn to trust in people and trust in the love I was receiving, and also to trust in the love I was trying to offer ... and, very slowly, I could feel the tectonic plates begin to shift.

Alongside that came a deeper affection for the things of this world. I began to be able to appreciate the spirit in nature; to celebrate the body, food, art, music; to see that everything was indeed an expression of the life force which lifts us up and helps us to take flight. Throughout that time, I continued the discipline of daily silence – not always; it was a custom more honoured in the breach than the observance, but the intention was there and I regularly managed to keep periods of silence, usually repeating a mantra.

As the years have gone by I have found new horizons beginning to open up. New ways of experiencing the world which resonate with the teachings of the great mystics. A sense, hard to describe, that there is another reality which can't be touched or named but lies just beyond the veil. A feeling that behind what we can see and touch and taste and hear is a place where nothing can be seen or touched or tasted or heard because nothing exists in any sense that we can understand – but there is a groundedness, a reality that is more solid than anything which surrounds us in the world of appearances. I have found that a gradual letting-go-ness – Meister Eckhart, whom we will meet later, uses the word *gelâzenheit* – seems to make it easier to touch the untouchable world and grasp the ungraspable truths that cannot be spoken or contained.

This is the exploration I've taken with Henry, Francesca and Deepti and many others. It has changed my life. The chapters that follow are a distillation of what I've learned.

2

Where are we now?

Shanon and I went to Norwich for a weekend away. Wandering round the great Norman cathedral, we found strange scratches on the walls just to the right of the high altar, and wondered what they might denote. A knowledgeable guide came to our aid. 'Those days, it was OK to draw on the walls of churches,' she told us. 'The nave of every church was the laity's area – the chancel was kept for the clergy. People used to come here and draw or write their prayers, or scratch thanksgivings on the wall if their prayers had been answered.'

'This one looks like a rune,' said Shanon, pointing towards a strange cross-like form with a carved triangle on top.

'That's the Trinity, with the cross standing for Jesus,' said the guide. 'And look, here are the names of people who must have died being remembered – Samuel Willion and Sarah Brakespeare – and these arrows are votive, they symbolize prayers.'

'So religion was much more demotic then,' I said. Shanon, the sociologist of religion, said: 'It's no less demotic now. You'd be surprised how many people pray. They just don't do it in church.'

That encounter with the popular religion of 800 years ago set me thinking about the parallels and discontinuities between the mediaeval church and us, in London, in the twenty-first century. The scholar Eamonn Duffy writes movingly in *The Stripping of the Altars*[4] of the responsibility men and women took for the altars and shrines that filled English churches until the Reformation. The embroidering and cleaning of altar linen, the provision of candles for Masses to be said daily for the souls of the dead. Pilgrimages to holy places, the cults of saints and their relics, miraculous healings and terrifying curses. Graffiti on the walls of churches was a witness to the power of prayer as well as a more mundane expression of community life, curses and damnations, the outworking of neighbourly squabbles or inter-villein rows.

There was much fragility. This was a world dependent on nature for its survival, with no illusions about the tenuousness of life. The danger of famine was ever present. A more efficient plough in the eighth and ninth centuries had increased yields, but most communities were still only one failed harvest away from famine, and although the increased yield enabled market towns to grow, they were very dependent on their immediate hinterland. A natural disaster or a hard winter could harm the whole population.

But there was also abundance. The rivers were full of fish and the forests held plenty of game. A good harvest meant a satisfactory, albeit hard, winter, and when the spring came there was real delight and renewed joy. Chaucer captures it in the richness and bawdiness of *The Canterbury Tales*.

Mediaeval Europe is often seen as a dark and hopeless period between the glories of Rome and the leap of progress that we call the Enlightenment. A time of squalor and disease, when humanity – at least at the European edge of the Asian world (where trade and culture thrived) – struggled with ignorance and hunger. The church ruled the roost in league with robber kings and feudal lords, and misery stalked the earth.

This perception of the centuries between 900 and 1400 is both partial and inaccurate. The people living then did not of course see themselves as 'mediaeval'. Life was lived on the cusp between the past and the future just as it is now. The known world was smaller, but there was much travel and interchange between cultures and communities. The church was a Europe-wide institution with Latin as its lingua franca and clergy and religious often moved from jurisdiction to jurisdiction.

True, Europe at the time had little to commend it to the peoples clustered along the Silk Road. Raiders from the East who made their way towards Europe in the centuries between 400 and 1000 CE, the Mongols and their like, chose to go south to Egypt rather than west into Germania and France, for there was little to be gained by invading such a backward part of the world. But the people of Europe thought, fought, created, dreamed and feared just as we do now, trying to make sense of a cosmos which seemed at times to be implacably set against them and at other times to be glowing with benevolence and light.

The boundaries between what is visible and what is invisible were thought to be porous. The spirits of good and evil dwelt nearby in the liminal spaces between the seen and the unseen. The cycle of the year was full of rites and rituals, acknowledging and placating these neighbouring spirits.

For example, the beating of the bounds of the parish, known as Rogation and taking place in the late spring, had a dual purpose. Ancient pagan fertility rituals merged with Christian observance. The whole community walked together around the parish boundary. Carrying sticks, they beat the ground. Sometimes children were beaten too, symbolically – not to hurt but as a way of impressing upon them where their boundaries lay. The walk was a kind of pilgrimage, partly to ensure that the members of the village, especially children, were aware of where their own parish ended and another's began, but more to seek God's forgiveness for the failings and sins of the community so that God would bless the harvest, and to wake the spirits of the earth so that they would nourish the seed. Every member of the village had to take part, for otherwise how could all harmful wickedness be exorcised?

I'm drawn to the mediaeval period because of that mingling of the now and the beyond. The twelfth and thirteenth centuries saw an upsurge in writings by people whom we now call mystics, although in those days they were simply seen as religious. We will meet some of them later: Meister Eckhart, Mother Julian, Ibn Arabi. They were all trying to put into words an experience of god that could not be described. They were pushing at the boundaries, drawing on the wisdom of previous centuries and speaking with remarkable similarity about what they were finding.

In the twelfth and thirteenth centuries people had not yet become embarrassed about naming the spiritual. Magic and mystery were all around, and much of life was spent trying to nourish the good and counter the evil. Magic wasn't about rabbits being produced from top hats at children's parties; magic was a part of life, a way of communicating with the good and evil spirits who were always present, just beyond the visible. It was a world of enchantment. Theology, the study of god, was the queen of the sciences because god was at the heart of everything, the foundation upon which everything else stood.

In the nineteenth century, sociologist Max Weber theorized that Europe in the modern era – and by extension the Western world – is a society where religion has lost its power because of a process of disenchantment. Mystery has been vanquished by the rationalism of the Enlightenment, by scientific method with its requirement for verifiability, by the materialism of capitalism. According to Weber and many since we live in a disenchanted world.

But Weber's narrative is being challenged. In *The Myth of Disenchantment*, the scholar of religion Jacob Josephson-Storm says:

> The single most familiar story in the history of science is the tale of disenchantment – of magic's exit from the henceforth law-governed world. I am here to tell you that as broad cultural history, this narrative is wrong.[5]

The disenchantment narrative, the triumph of materialism, capitalism and consumerism – the three great isms of our time, entangled with empire, whiteness and maleness – has impoverished Western society and brought the natural world close to nemesis, but throughout the centuries spiritual exploration has never stopped. The enchantment has never really gone away. Josephson-Storm writes that even such supposed rationalists as Isaac Newton and Sigmund Freud were immersed in the occult. Magic and the occult are as present now as they ever were but they have been pushed to the margins.

I am sure that the decline in religious observance in Europe is a by-product of the way the spiritual quest has been sidelined. Theology is no longer the queen of the sciences, and we are the poorer for it.

I'm not a Luddite. I like flush toilets and antibiotics as much as anyone. But I am sure that human experience is massively enriched by a serious exploration of the life of the spirit, and we would be in a better place if we listened more carefully to what the spirit is saying to the world.

Precisely because the spiritual is beyond the rational, it can be very disorientating – but that is one of its benefits. The spiritual path calls into question all that we think is certain, just as quantum physics calls into question all that we thought Newtonian physics tells us about solidity and immutability – and time. As we know from Einstein, time is not fixed. It's relative. Time and space bend. So I find it helpful to think of different kinds of time:

- Linear time, which is how we mark the passing of the years – treating time as a straight line, from the past to the future, and in which moments are unrepeatable.
- Cyclical time, the time of seasons and the rotation of the earth.
- Cosmic time, the interlocking times of stars and nebulae and galaxies.
- God's time, the time of the spirit, which is outside and beyond anything we can conceive or understand but which contains everything.

The spiritual journey takes us across fragile and fleeting bridges between linear time, cyclical time, cosmic time and god's time. It seeks a deeper understanding of the intersection between the present and the infinite. It takes us into a world where what seemed certain turns out to be tentative, and what seemed tentative and indefinable turns out to be more real than we can imagine. By daring to let go of our certainties we undermine the supposed binary between proveability and mystery. We reopen the conversation between the material and the spiritual. By leaving behind the scaffolding on which we hang our identity we can take flight into a new world where there is everything to play for.

Religious traditions, both Eastern and Western, often share a core principle – to find ourselves we must first lose ourselves. Deny yourself, says Jesus, take up your cross and follow me. The

Buddha calls us to leave desire behind, because only by ending desire can we discover truth.

But it's easier said than done. Identity is a hard-won thing, especially in a world where there are so many power dynamics complicating the picture. Expectations around gender, race and sexuality – patriarchy, whiteness, straightness – bear a toxicity which is insidious and destructive. The identities we work out for ourselves respond to layer upon layer of societal pressures, whether we are men, women, black, brown, abled or disabled, straight, queer, rich or poor. To deny ourselves we have to understand who we are – to know our authentic selves – and this is a huge challenge when so much of our self-awareness is defined by the pressures and demands of the society around us. There is a process of taking hold and letting go, and, in my experience, it is often the people most on the margins who are most engaged in the spiritual quest.

I will return to this later. For now, it's enough to say that it is not a coincidence that so many queer people are, in spite of centuries of oppression and marginalization by religious institutions, persistent seekers of deep spirituality. Just as the journey takes us beyond the everyday limitations of time and space, so it pushes at the boundaries of what is 'normal' in society. Queerness resists categorization.

We live in a world caught between a craving for certainty and a passion for diversity. Powerful men (nearly always men) take control of political systems and nations, imposing their worldviews: Make America Great Again; invading Ukraine to build Greater Russia. At the same time, queer people assert with determination their right to exist, which is producing a determined push-back from white patriarchy. Queerness in its deepest sense is about challenging the concept of 'normal'. It takes us beyond routine categories into a new world where nothing is quite as it seems, and new relationships and new ways of life emerge. It's for everyone, not just LGBTQI+ people. Queerness is not just about sexuality or gender. According to Charlie Bell in his book *Queer Redemption*, it's about 'putting a stumbling block in the way of the status quo':

'Normativity' is a blasphemous attempt to replace God-given diversity with comfortable human categories.[6]

Queering is about discovering a deeper, often disruptive, reality behind apparent certainties, a reality that resonates with the spiritual quest because queerness is beyond definition, beyond stasis, open to experience. It speaks of the glorious complexity of nature and humanity to which we are all invited.

***

How are we to live well? What does human flourishing truly look like? How do we live a good life? Not necessarily a valuable life – the maverick Catholic theologian and priest Ivan Illich speaks of the insidiousness of replacing the notion of goodness, which is absolute, with value, which is relative. So the question is not, 'Where do I find value?' But, 'How do I find goodness in my life?'

Deepti asked that question from her Hindu background. Francesca was wondering how to reconcile the strictness of her Catholic upbringing with her continued yearning for understanding. Henry wanted answers to his questions; a sense of connection or completeness.

My reply to each of them was 'Bring it on!' Bring on the mystery, bring on the haziness, bring on the shadows and the brightness, bring on the stories and the narratives, bring on the questions, bring on the cloud of unknowing, bring on the journey into lands where boundaries are blurred, the mountains fade into valleys and the valleys into the infinite horizon.

One last question. We live in a world of deep pain and enormous suffering, where death is an all too stark reality and the fragility of nature is terrifyingly apparent. What about pain? What about suffering? How can we make sense of a world that contains so many tragedies and so much destruction?

We can't hide from the pain within ourselves or the pain of the world. We will find companions on the road who have anguish in their eyes, who are one step away from misery, who are carrying demons on their backs. How do we incorporate that pain, that fear, those traumas – not to diminish its awfulness but to learn to understand the words of Psalm 139:

> If I say, 'Surely the darkness shall cover me,
>   and the light around me become night,'
> even the darkness is not dark to you;
>   the night is as bright as the day. (Ps. 139.11–12)

How do we reach across the void and respond to the flickers of new life we see in the lives of the others we meet in this wilderness we call the earth? How can we learn to live well in a world of loss and fear? Listen to the wisdom of the Islamic scholar, mystic and poet, Jalāl al-Dīn Muḥammad Rūmī:

> I said: What about my eyes?
> He said: Keep them on the road.
>
> I said: What about my passion?
> He said: Keep it burning.
>
> I said: What about my heart?
> He said: Tell me what you hold inside it?
> I said: Pain and sorrow.
> He said: Stay with it.
> The wound is the place where the Light enters you.

3

How did we get here?

I've been vicar of St John's for more than 15 years. It's an exciting place to work and live. The community gathered around the church is both extraordinary, because every community is extraordinary, and resolutely ordinary, drawing its members from across the spectrum of London's population.

St John's is at a crossroads. Geographically and metaphorically. The church is at the south end of Waterloo Bridge, where a main road leads towards south London and another follows the bank of the Thames. The roundabout between us and Waterloo Station houses the biggest cinema screen in Britain, the BFI Imax. The station is one of the busiest in the country. We have the National Theatre, the Southbank Centre, Shell's head offices and King's College, London, close by. We are a place of transition; millions of people travel by or near the church each day.

All sorts of things happen at St John's – community projects, English language classes for people who have recently arrived in the UK, concerts, conferences, exhibitions. Many people come to the building. Relatively few come to worship, but we try to be a place of stability. We've been here for 200 years. There is a richness in the place we inhabit, the stable and constantly evolving congregation that comes on Sunday to sing hymns, pray and worship, the light we try to offer in a world where light is scarce.

We attract. People in transition, people arriving in London, people looking for something. We attract the lost and the lonely, the liminal, the learned and the left behind. We draw in people who have an inchoate desire for something, they know not what, that comes under the general heading of god.

All communities are webs of connections. The threads that bind them are complex. At St John's we have some deep and lasting links which are maintained from year to year: people who have been coming through the doors on a Sunday morning since the 1960s, people who remember the church when the churchyard outside was a mass of tents occupied by homeless people, people for whom this part of London has been home for generations.

But these are in a minority now. The threads that bind us are more tenuous than they were. The cost of housing locally is out of reach for nearly everyone, unless they are lucky enough to be allocated one of the cooperative or council or housing association homes. For most, the best that can be hoped for is a nearly unaffordable space for a year or so, too ephemeral to be a place for plans to be made or roots to be sunk. So now, increasingly, we draw people to us who are travelling from places where the rents are marginally less unaffordable, from Peckham or Balham or Mile End – thank God for the Tube and the quiet of Sunday morning streets for the buses that bring our congregation.

The web of the city is intensely fragile. London is still recovering from the effects of the Covid-19 pandemic. Young people, especially, are reporting an increase in loneliness. There are fewer stable jobs and a dramatic increase in temporary or gig work. London and the UK have not found their place yet in the aftermath of Brexit. I am acutely aware of the fragility of the lives of many people in their twenties and thirties.

All this is against a backdrop of authoritarian government around the world, triumphant consumerism, the re-eruption of war in Europe, the latest iteration of war in Israel/Palestine and so many other places in the world – and the underbass of climate change as spring gets earlier and maximum temperature and rainfall records are each year made and broken.

Insecure work. The coming of Artificial Intelligence. An erupting gap between rich and poor, billionaires taking control of the narrative and most media. An inchoate anger which is whipped up and exploited by those who paint a vision of a nostalgic past where migration was rare and jobs plentiful, food abundant and everything was cheap. People hear a story of dispossession, from the land they consider theirs, from the jobs they thought were theirs, from the housing that they believed was their right, and they believe it and act on it. Seeking security in nationalistic identity. Seeking safety in numbers. The world is a frightening place at the moment, whether you live in London, Lagos or Lima.

The barricades have been raised. Identification by label, the creation of social media silos, misinformation and fake news are outworkings of an underlying fear that seeks comfort in a falsely nostalgic identity. That, combined with a belief that wealth really does bring happiness (the triumph of consumerism, the gospel of Capital), creates boundaries and divisions which are becoming more intransigent. The right-wing populist narrative is that for you to succeed, someone else has to fail, and for you to win, someone else has to lose.

Climate change and ecological breakdown may seem to be a long way down the list of priorities of people who are worrying about the next meals for their family, but I'm convinced that the prospect of climate catastrophe adds to the sense of insecurity and fear that builds unbreachable walls where before there were porous hedges.

Francesca, Deepti and Henry were living the fragility of the city. Henry came to London with some ready-made connections; he arrived from university in Durham and some of his cohort came to the city with him. Francesca, less so; she was here for a year, possibly more, to complete a Master's degree and then perhaps a PhD. Deepti came from Leicester where she had been at university. Not many of her friends came with her, and most of her family is in Leicester or in Hyderabad. All three were searching for something that would give them the beginning of a sense of home – structure, community.

It's not only young people who are searching. I have many conversations with people in their forties and fifties, wondering where to find solid ground; and those of us in our sixties and more are trying to make sense of it all, when we have grandchildren and great-nephews and great-nieces emerging blinking into the world. What are we leaving the generations who will tread the streets after us?

* * *

But lurking beneath all this I have an unsettling sense of doubt. Am I guilty of failing to see the positive? London is alive, the streets are full, the restaurants seem to be flourishing, there is overflowing choice; the shops are full of beautiful things to buy at reasonable prices, tourists crowd around the gates of Buckingham Palace, the galleries are full of remarkable exhibitions. For many, money is more abundant than it has ever been. Why should we worry? Shouldn't we eat, drink and be merry, for tomorrow we die?

The philosopher Charles Taylor, in his book *A Secular Age*, reflects on how society has changed, and asks how and why we seem to be living in a time when God and spirituality are more marginalized than they have ever been. He unrolls a process that started in the thirteenth century, away from a society where God is in charge and has the power to create or destroy, to bless or to damn, towards a society where each person is uniquely in their own individual sphere: the outworking of scientific materialism and the marginalization of the spiritual.

Weber's theory of disenchantment is a response – albeit oversimplified – to this dominant strand of thought. Influential forces have embraced the narrative of liberation from superstition – secular liberalism has certainly opened up new ways of being which have brought many benefits, not least in terms of human rights – but the downside has been what Taylor speaks of as the 'buffered self':

> I claim that the coming of modern secularity has been coterminous with the rise of a purely self-sufficient humanism – e.g. a humanism accepting no goals beyond human flourishing.[7]

Human flourishing is, you will say, a good thing – but that begs the question of what kind of flourishing? Increasingly, human flourishing as conceived by our politicians and media leaves little space for the inexplicable, the transcendent, the spiritual. Even where religion's writ continues to run, power lies with organizations that refuse contradiction and offer unchallengeable levels of certainty – the Christian right in the USA and so many fundamentalist expressions of other religious traditions.

HOW DID WE GET HERE?

I'm sure that the rise in populist and autocratic government around the world is in part a result of the buffered individualism that Charles Taylor describes, coopting a version of religion that puts me before you and nation before god. Spiritual motifs are brought into play to create a superficial depth. Look at the perverting of Christianity in the rituals of the Ku Klux Klan or the QAnon Shaman who was one of the leaders of the assault on Capitol Hill on 6 January 2021.

Religion and spirituality as agents of oppression and hate can never be good. But if, in leaving behind oppressive forms of religion and spirituality, we also leave behind the ways humans have made sense of the universe and have learnt to love, to give, to be transformed, then we commit a serious error. The world is suffering the consequences.

Spirit matters. It matters because human experience is complex and beautiful, simple and ugly. Our hearts are lifted by the space beyond the stars, but the depth of infinity holds terrors. We are moved by love, energized by fear, gripped by hate, transformed by joy. Where did life come from, why does the cosmos exist, how can I make sense of my place in it, why am I here? The answer given by buffered individualism is this: just because. The answer given by those who are seeking spiritual wisdom is more complex. It acknowledges the paradox of life, the mystery of love and the unknowable truths at the core of our existence.

Spirituality is subversive. It's not a coincidence that the great spiritual leaders and teachers, almost without exception, embraced poverty and simplicity. Their teachings and their lives undermine the foundations of materialism, consumerism and capitalism. The growth for which Jesus and Muhammad call is spiritual, not material. The radical equality of all in the face of infinite love, powerfully expressed in the story of Jesus washing his disciples' feet (John 13.1–7), breaks the vicious circle of economic growth at any cost by refusing the harsh reality of exploitation.

So come with me down this road less travelled. It's a road that needs discernment and time, so that the wheat of nourishment can be sorted from the chaff of superficiality. In Part 2 of this book, we will pass through places marked Creation,

Bodies, Nature, Justice, Lament, Death, Light. We'll start with the big picture – the act of creation and why creativity matters for the spiritual journey. Then we'll focus on our bodies, too often undervalued. We'll look at nature and the cosmos, and think about how our spirits are nourished by connecting with the natural world. The buffered self is a destructive notion; no one is an island and everyone is equally loved, so working for justice is a vital part of the path. If we are to live truly, we can't escape from the pain of the world; lament brings necessary wisdom. The only event of which we can be certain, death, comes next; how do we live with the knowledge of our imminent demise? Finally, we go into the light which is the ultimate goal of the journey.

I will draw on many spiritual traditions because, as I said to the person who sent me the complaining email, god is bigger than the church. I focus on Christianity because that's what I know best, but I am for ever grateful that my partner Shanon is Muslim. He has opened up the multilayered teachings of the Qur'an and the writings of Sufi saints and poets. It would be foolish and counterproductive to limit ourselves to Christianity when there are galaxies of wisdom and experience across the centuries – from the earliest reflections of the philosophers of China, India and Greece, through the teachings of the Tantra, of the Kabbala and Sufism, and much more, right up to the present day.

In Part 3, I will ask you to forget everything you have read in Part 2. We'll delve into the wisdom of the mystics, to whom the only real truth is that god is no-thing, and nothing can be said or thought or done which will bring us closer to god. It's a huge paradox, the greatest of many paradoxes that we will encounter on our path, but I'm sure grasping the mystical language of unsaying is the only way towards the dazzling darkness at the heart of everything.

It's complicated! There will be challenges, trials and tribulations on this pilgrim's progress. You may find yourself in the slough of despond. But, with perseverance, I promise you will find it rewarding. If you seek god you find god. At the centre of it all is the belief that we are all part of a reality that can't be spoken or contained: it is, in the words of the poet George Herbert, something understood.[8]

PART 2

How do we get there?

4

Exploring creation

In the winter of 2024 I went to several exceptional exhibitions in London. A collection of Vincent Van Gogh's work from 1888–89 – 'Poets and Lovers' – was shown at the National Gallery. The exhibition focused on the paintings and drawings he made in the south of France. The artist was pushing at the boundaries of painting. The vibrancy of his paint, whether he's depicting an olive grove or a poet, speaks of the realm beyond the visible. I have a soft spot for olive trees – gnarled and twisted silver-grey trunks scrabbling out of dry land laden with the scent of the Mediterranean. Van Gogh takes an ordinary olive grove and, through paint and light and vision, transforms it into a dynamic celebration of life in nature, the sap rising, the spirit speaking.

Another remarkable collection was shown at the Courtauld Institute. The pictures made by Monet, many from a suite of rooms in the Savoy Hotel just up the Thames from the Courtauld, spoke of his fascination – obsession? – with the smog of London. Unlike his water lily paintings with their cascades of reds and purples and greens, these are yellow, sickly, the sun obscured by the thick toxicity of London's air, weighed down by the fumes of tramp steamers and coal smoke from a million chimneys. Darkness and destruction were at the heart of the richest city in the world, the ever-flowing river scarcely visible beyond the fumes of fog.

At the same time, the Victoria and Albert Museum mounted an exhibition of art from India from the time of the Mughal emperors – Akbar, Jehangir, Shah Jehan. They retained artists and craftspeople in their courts, making drawings and artefacts which speak of the majesty of the Mughal courts and the depth of the spiritual life of the region. There were beautiful ceramics and fabrics and wonderful jewellery, skilfully created with love and delight. Akbar wanted to encourage respect between the communities in India – Hindu, Sikh, Buddhist, Muslim and, with the arrival of the Portuguese, Christian. He commissioned Persian translations of the great Sanskrit Hindu texts – the Ramayana and the Harivamsa – and translations of the life of Christ into Persian, all sumptuously decorated and illustrated.

Craft. Art. Mystery. The potter and spiritual director Annette Kaye says that art emerges from the impulse to give expression to our yearnings, to connect us to the depths of our humanity and to stretch us towards the transcendent. The painter Leonora Carrington said: 'There are things that are not sayable, and that is why we have art.' That resonates with a definition of spiritual direction: 'Two people sitting in a room talking about what can't be talked about.'

The spiritual journey and the creative journey both need commitment and conviction. Artists and craftspeople build skills and portfolios over decades. Families of painters in the fourteenth and fifteenth centuries passed on skills from father to son or, more rarely, mother to daughter – Orazio and Artemisia Gentileschi, the Bellinis in Venice, the Ghirlandaios – learning their trade but always pushing at the boundaries to try to express the truths behind the stories. Christ's crucifixion. The cleansing of the Temple. The woman taken in adultery.

As well as commitment and conviction and learnt skills, spirit and creation both need surrender of control. I am sure that everyone has the potential for creativity. I try to unlock mine by nurturing a community in Waterloo and writing books about spirituality. I learn from artists and from my own experience that it requires self-denial. A point comes when putting one word behind the next is not the result of ordered planning but of openness to the unexpected, surrendering to the depths of spirituality or creativity which like icebergs glitter above the waters of daily life.

They both need respect for *stuff*. In the first chapters of Genesis, God is both a worker in clay and a seamstress. God forms Adam out of the dust of the earth, and after he and Eve have eaten the fruit of the Tree of Knowledge God makes clothes for them. The earth, this astonishing ball of molten lava surrounded by rocks, water and air, is the bedrock of the transcendent world in which we live. Creativity and spiritual exploration can't exist in a vacuum. They require the earthiness of clay and the mutability of water, the glory of gold and the interstices of atomic physics to speak. We are stardust for a moment coalesced into flesh and blood; mud people looking at the stars. Art speaks of the transcendent, and the world and the heavens stop to listen.

But surely this is all absurdly highfalutin? Isn't creativity really just about telling a story or making nice things? Think of Netflix series, *Game of Thrones*, *Succession*, or figurines of cats and dogs ('Make more cats and dogs,' said a friend of Annette's, 'they sell better') – are these really trying to express the voice of the transcendent?

The Nigerian novelist Chinua Achebe said:

> Art is a person's constant effort to create for himself a different order of reality from that which is given to him.[9]

Religious historian Diana Butler Bass of the Centre for Action and Contemplation, wrote:

> The Spirit is the driving force, the animating creative life of the entire cosmos, responsible, in particular, for the vision of those in human history most attuned to the heartbeat of God.[10]

In the moment of creation, the artist is seeking to communicate something that is beyond words. I look at a picture or listen to a piece of music and I'm inspired by the glimpse I am given into the artist's heart. Monet, wrestling over the depiction of alien and inhumane smog, or Mughal artists depicting Krishna in a Persian tradition, or the chords and melodies of a toccata and fugue by Bach – all these are secret gifts concealed in plain sight, gifts that need an openness to be received. Whether it's the awesome majesty of a fugue as architectural as a Gothic cathedral, or the mucky biliousness of oil paint depicting a London fog, or the counterintuitive blueness of the god Krishna, each needs assent both from the creator, who is offering something deep of themselves, and from the viewer, who is opening themselves up to receive the offering.

Perhaps music is the clearest expression of this process. I think of the gargantuan symphonies of Anton Bruckner, a deeply engaged Catholic, building a sculpture of the cosmos, a mountainscape of peaks and troughs rolling through time. I listen to them in the comfort of my living room and when I allow myself to be open, my heart resonates with the drama of the huge chords rolling in like waves from the depths of Bruckner's heart.

For you, there will be something else. Maybe the desert harmonies of kora music from sub-Saharan cultures, griots harmonizing on the themes of generations of courtly music in Mali, or the visionary hip-hop of Kendrick Lamarr, or the raga tradition in India stretching out across time and space to communicate in music what the Mahabharata speaks of in epic words, or maybe songwriters like Taylor Swift, Billie Eilish or Sufjan Stevens.

It's the product of work and re-work, vision and re-vision. Creativity is a way to cross boundaries, especially the artificial boundary between the physical and the spiritual. I look at a drawing of a group of men fighting by Leonardo, say, or a picture of people in a Persian garden, and I know that I am being asked to think of the brutality of war or of an earthly paradise.

The symbolism of two burnt nails placed together to form a cross, or the sinuous calligraphy of a verse from the Qur'an, or the carefully placed stones in a dry landscape garden in Kyoto – they all speak of the infinite spaces between things. They are ways of crystalizing the mystery, the dot beneath the Arabic word B in the word Bismillah which, said Ali the cousin of the Prophet Muhammad, contains the whole cosmos and all wisdom (see p. 112).

Creativity and spirituality invite us to look behind the veil of the temple and see into the unseeable beyond. Both are asking questions, both recognize the truth that nothing is quite what it seems. 'I am not sure of what I see,' said Alberto Giacometti, 'it is too complex.' His stick-thin figures come out of the alienation and loss of World War Two; he forces the clay into figures that expand our understanding of what it means to be human. Loneliness alongside loneliness.

Remember that you are dust and to dust you shall return. At our first Exploring Spirit session at St John's, Annette brought sacks of clay and gave each of us a lump. We were invited to use the clay as we pleased. There was a delightful diversity of little sculptures, from Japanese buddhas to a stable and horses to my rather misshapen foot. My clay wanted to become a foot, I decided, as that is what it became.

Annette spoke of imbari – a sacred ritual in communities in Africa, often carried out at times of fear, as part of the worship of Ala, the earth goddess. Imbari is the moment when members of the community gather together whatever they have made or whatever they want to make as an offering. Once gathered, the offerings are abandoned for sun and wind and rain to consume, slowly or quickly, until everything's gone. It is a holy collaboration of the community, a moment of solidarity, but in its ephemerality it speaks of the fragility of the world in which we live.

We created a tiny imbari with our works in clay, and looked at it, and saw that it was good. And then we left the pieces we had made. Annette took them away and reworked them, and the imbari was no more.

I love the sense that the moment of creation passes. We take recordings for granted now but there was a time when the only music available was live music, and it vanished as soon as it had been heard. The great landscapes of sound composed over the centuries only existed at the moment when they were being played by an orchestra and heard by an audience. Even works designed to last decay or disappear – 'Look on my works, ye mighty, and despair'[11] – and pieces that are there for a season and then gone, such as the work of sculptors in nature like Andy Goldsworthy with his collations of autumn leaves, have a powerful resonance. Nothing lasts, but it did exist for a second, for a millisecond, for now.

A paradox of spirituality is that it too is an absent presence, fleeting, untouchable, uncatchable, but there like the wind on a Van Gogh cornfield. A few years ago, dreamcatchers were everywhere, those fragile creations of thread and beads which hung by windows to catch dreams as they passed. Moments of prayer are exactly that, just moments. For those who try to keep silence, who have periods of silence for ten or 20 minutes or an hour, during those periods, I think, for most people, the moments of self-forgetting or of transcendence are vanishingly few.

It's about the nature of time: linear, cyclical, cosmic, god's time. We are reaching for a deeper understanding of the connection between the now and the infinite. Art and spirituality create bridges between the momentary and the timeless – different kinds of bridges. Creativity is about unexpected connections. Different materials, objects, visions are brought together to form new kinds of meaning. Tracey Emin's bed, that notorious sculpture, spoke about her life – it captured a moment that depicted her situation at the time she made the work. Or Bruckner making rivers of sound, or Annette's pots speaking of the spirit within them. Or Japanese animée, the much-loved Studio Ghibli films, *Howl's Moving Castle*, *Spirited Away* ... a magic flying castle, malign spirits who turn parents into pigs because of their greed. Fiction gains much of its power from the blurring of boundaries, from telling stories that include the unexpected jolt, the plot twist, the combination of mystery and tangibility; Terry Pratchett merrily combining the fantastic and the everyday in his flights of fancy such as *Small Gods*, an extended reflection on the nature of faith and a great story.

Creativity and spirituality are playful, too. I love these verses from Psalm 104:

> O Lord, how manifold are your works!
>   In wisdom you have made them all;
>   the earth is full of your creatures.
> Yonder is the sea, great and wide,
>   creeping things innumerable are there,
>   living things both small and great.
> There go the ships,
>   and Leviathan that you formed to sport. (Ps. 104.24–26)

In art we can create a world that is not the world we know, a better, a more frightening, a funnier or a darker world. A world where clay speaks of dragons, or where the key of D minor, the key of Mozart's *Requiem*, speaks of death.

Listen, are you breathing just a little, and calling it a life?[12]

Creativity destabilizes. It opens up new vistas. It makes landscapes out of impasto and oil and canvas and twisted metal and bombed-out plaster, which speak of destruction or hope or a cocktail of the two. Spirituality too. Nothing is quite as it seems. So I encourage you to own your creativity and let it speak into your spiritual journey. Whatever inspires you, whatever lifts you up, wherever you see unexpected connections or find moments of joy, of reflection, of darkness; these are what take us into a world that is both questing and questioning. We can use our bodies, our hearts and our minds to explore, combining ingredients unexpectedly to create something beautiful or challenging or fun, something that helps us to play our part in the infinite cosmos. So let's think, now, about how bodies speak into spirit and spirit into bodies.

5

Exploring bodies

'I look at my children,' said Laych, 'and I'm in awe. I see what they're doing, how they're growing, who they're becoming, and I think, "Anh and I made those!" The feeling I really have is wonder.'

'Wonder at what?' I asked.

'Wonder at these people we're creating, all three of them, their tiny bodies coming out of me. How they grow and become more themselves every day. It makes me cry!'

The search for life. Spacecraft and telescopes scanning the universe for faint radio signals that might signify the presence of other bodies elsewhere in the cosmos. Anxiously analysing the spectrometry of impossibly distant planets to see if their atmospheres contain gases that might be evidence we are not alone. The long debate about how life originated on earth; how chemical reactions produced proteins which produced, over millions of years, single-cell organisms, which, over further millions of years, combined and began to diversify, and developed ways of reproducing that were resilient and reliable, so that single-cell organisms could multiply and complexify, and, over further billions of years, could evolve and adapt and grow and fight and learn and struggle and love and, ultimately, produce the children of Laych and Anh, who can already ask the question, 'If god made the universe, who made god?' and whose being fills Laych with wonder and makes her cry.

There's a word for it – a contested word. I know, very well, the arguments that tell us, in a universe of between 200 billion and 2 trillion galaxies (nobody really knows), each containing millions of planets, it is predictable that one planet in a tiny corner of an obscure galaxy might have the right conditions for life to emerge. That argument makes sense to me and I can't gainsay it, but that doesn't stop me thinking that the reality of life, the living, breathing flesh and bone and arteries and lymphatic ducts and skin and fingernails and braincells which are at this moment working together to produce this sentence are the product of a process which, whether logical or not, is best described as miraculous.

A miracle: the word derives from the Latin *miraculum*, meaning 'object of wonder'. A miracle doesn't necessarily require divine agency. We can say that the emergence of life is an outcome of random processes which, by some extraordinary chance, combined to create organic matter capable of placing itself in relation to infinity and asking the question, 'Why am I here?', and we can still call it a miracle.

Or, to use another word, a mystery. A mystery is a question that cannot be solved, or a question to which the solution is hidden: the question, for example, 'Why is there something rather than nothing?', or the question, 'Why does life exist?' It's a question to which this book is trying to offer a possible answer, although the definitive answer has already been provided by Douglas Adams in *The Hitchhiker's Guide to the Galaxy*: '42'.[13]

We know, now, that there is continuity between organic and inorganic matter – between hearts and stones – because both are made up of atoms which are made up of tiny quantum bursts of energy, powered by miniscule electrical charges. I and the table at which I sit are one. But the table doesn't think – or at least, I think it doesn't think – and I am the thing that enables the table to be conceived as a table rather than a random collection of molecules and atoms that happens to have four legs and a flat top. I can name the table, I can name the galaxies, I can name the plants and animals, I can name god. I can relate to you through the pages of this book, I can relate to Shanon through making him a coffee, I can relate to other humans because they can relate to me, and so it continues, from generation to generation.

I can do all this because I am embodied. The human body is the greatest miracle of all. It is uniquely complex and astonishingly adaptable. It can invent electronic intelligence which will, we are told, soon be beyond human understanding. It can, most of the time, fend off illnesses and take corrective action to avoid threats. It can laugh, smile, cry, shout, eat, drink, be merry and create wonderful children who make Laych cry.

So why has the body been so mistrusted by faith traditions? Why is the life of the spirit so often seen as opposed to the life of the flesh? Why have women's bodies and queer bodies and trans bodies and black bodies and disabled bodies so often been wantonly oppressed, broken or destroyed? Why are sexuality and gender such toxic subjects, and why are atypical relationships so often under attack?

It's been this way for a long time. The first of the Four Noble Truths of the Buddha, originating in the fifth century BCE, is that the perceivable world is dukkha (pain) – and the third Noble Truth is that the pain of existence can only be overcome through letting go of desire. The ultimate goal for Hindus is for the atman (soul) to merge with Brahman, the ultimate reality, within which there is no differentiation and which is utterly beyond the physical. Christianity and Islam, and, to a lesser extent, Judaism, have at their core the belief in a heaven and hell that can only be accessed after liberation from this world through death, and the thing that constrains us, holding us captive and gluing us to the material world, is the human body.

The trouble is this: the body is dangerous.

> Human flesh is always traversing and transgressing boundaries; its fluids seeping out, its skin touching other skins, its limbs entangling aliens – human and divine. It leaves one land and enters another.[14]

The rules set out in the book of Leviticus are a purity code. Their aim is to keep the priesthood of the Israelites pure by separating them from all that is unclean or polluting. It's not just food. Bodies that transgress boundaries are also dangerous. Anthropologist Mary Douglas, in her influential book *Purity and Danger*, defines dirt as 'matter out of place'. Leviticus is palpable in its distaste for people with blemishes, for small people, for menstruating women, for men who have sex with men as with a woman.

The body is always at risk of pollution. It is also a pollutant, and, in the Levitical code, women's bodies are a particular threat. The prophet Ezekiel uses misogynistic language to describe the behaviour of Jerusalem, and the book of Proverbs is full of warnings about the doom that awaits men who succumb to the blandishments of women. Eve, of course, is the instigator of the rebellion against God's commands: 'The woman ... gave me fruit from the tree, and I ate' (Gen. 3.12) – which is the start of all the trouble.

In the New Testament, St Paul regularly draws a distinction between *sarx* (flesh) and *psyche* (spirit). He appears to mistrust the physical, the here and now. He wrote to the Philippians:

> For our conversation is in heaven; from whence also we look for the Saviour, the Lord Jesus Christ: Who shall change our vile body, that it may be fashioned like unto his glorious body, according to the working whereby he is able even to subdue all things unto himself. (Phil. 3.20–21, AV)

The phrase 'vile bodies' has found its way into common English speech, even though the original Greek has overtones more of humility and earthiness than of the nastiness implied by the word 'vile'.

Mortification of the flesh is associated with saints and seers. St Jerome (c.342–420) was one of many early Christians who extolled virginity as the very highest form of Christian living, safeguarding believers against the pollution of sex. He speaks of wrestling with his demons:

> Although in my fear of hell I had consigned myself to this prison [the desert] where I had no companions but scorpions and wild beasts, I often found myself amid bevvies of girls. My face was pale and frame chilled with fasting; yet my mind was burning with desire.[15]

Those images of the Desert Fathers locking themselves away to wrestle with demons or flagellating themselves to kill their earthly passions; emaciated Sannyasin in India taming the lusts of the body through ascetic practices, surviving on a bowl of thin gruel and what fruits they can glean from the side of the road; the persecution of queer people, the denial of rights and roles to women – all these are outworkings of the fear of polluting, of impure bodies – usually, the non-straight, non-white, non-male bodies – which threaten the patriarchal and white hegemony under which Western society has been yoked for so long.

Power and sex. Policing desire. Who has held the power, in so many cultures across so many millenia? Men – straight men – who have demanded the exclusion of those who threaten their narrative and the control of those who might muddy the bloodline. Paternity relies on fidelity; a father needs to be confident that the child he is bringing up is his biological son to carry forward his legacy. So women and their bodies are corralled into subsidiary roles in a generational game of thrones. Queer people, those outside the norm, are potentially subversive too, so their bodies must be policed – and Western imperialism has turned black and brown people's bodies into objects for exploitation and sale.

Religion has always been a battleground for the conflict between spirit and matter. It still is, as those of us in the Church of England know only too well. The struggles over the inclusion of queer people are by no means over. The sexuality debate is particularly toxic because it touches on so many aspects of faith and spirituality: the interpretation of Scripture, the authority of history, the individual's relationship with God, sexual purity, the status of heterosexual marriage. There is not space here to rehearse those arguments. But I am transfixed by the crucifixion of desire in the name of purity, because this is where we find the heart of the matter.

When I was a fledgling Christian I was taught about the different kinds of love, as defined by the Greek words *agape*, *philia* and *eros*. *Agape* denotes selfless, unconditional love. *Philia* denotes the love between friends or siblings. *Eros* denotes romantic or passionate love. I was taught that *agape* and *philia* are good, pure kinds of love, but that *eros* is dangerous and should be shunned: proper spiritual love is unblemished by the temptations of erotic desire.

It's taken many years for me to understand that desire, *eros*, is a vital part of the spiritual journey. Literally vital, for desire is life-giving. A life-giving spirituality is one that is passionate and alive, that feels desire and responds to it. I am inspired by the sense that we are being drawn into a deeper life by a spirit which calls to us, which actively desires a relationship with us. I am inspired, too, by the notion that god's love is a love that, as well as being unconditional, deep and infinite, reaches out and is full of passion.

To be sure, desire is perilous. It can draw us into places of darkness and destruction. 'You shall have no other gods before me,' runs the first commandment. You shall have no idols. The body is often turned into an idol, the source and goal of unhealthy desire. We see it in the fetishizing of the body beautiful and the objectification of bodies in the worlds of fashion and pornography. But desire also opens up vistas of light. The glances that pass between two people in love are a delight. The spiritual journey is like dancing on a knife-edge. The body is the dancer.

Because desire is perilous, and because we humans are deeply fallible, there has been a long history of attempts to repress desire through social control or through extreme asceticism. (One of my favourite jokes: 'Why do puritans not have sex standing up?' 'Because it might lead to dancing.')

It didn't have to be like this. In the same centuries in which the Hebrew Bible and early Christian writings were developing a fortress of resistance to the blandishments of bodies, the Greeks and Romans were producing marvellous statues, startling in their celebration of the male and female form. Further east along the Silk Road, in India and China, faith traditions were developing a panoply of gods and enlightened beings celebrating physicality. In the earliest Sanskrit Scriptures, Devi – literally, the goddess – is the source of all creation, encompassing the entire cosmos, both matter and spirit. She is depicted in many forms, multi-armed, multi-headed and worshipped in heady festivals of colour, music and light.

In Buddhism, the relationship between spirit and body is much more nuanced than the concept that the world is *dukkha* might imply. The body – *rupa* – is one of the five *skandha* (attributes), which go to make up a person. The body, the mind and the spirit cannot be separated.

There is one thing, monks, that, cultivated and regularly practiced leads to a deep sense of urgency, to the supreme peace, to mindfulness and clear comprehension, to the attainment of right vision and knowledge, to happiness here and now, to realizing deliverance by wisdom and the fruition of Holiness: It is mindfulness of the body.[16]

In Hinduism, too, the body is to be treated as a temple; it is where the spirit dwells, and the processes of ritual cleansing, of yoga and meditation, of carefully managed diet, are how the physicality of flesh can be pressed into the service of the spiritual journey. To be sure, the aim is to break free of the cycle of death and rebirth, but the great seers teach that the goal is reached through caring for the body and enabling it to flourish so that the spiritual life can flourish too.

The word that is often translated as 'soul' in the Hebrew Scriptures, *nephesh*, has overtones of both soul and body. The word that is nearly always translated as 'spirit', *ruach*, also means breath, as does *pneuma* in Greek. Breath is what gives life to the body. In the book of Genesis, God the potter creates life by breathing into the clay out of which God has formed Adam – a compound of two Hebrew words meaning blood and ground. Rabbinistic and kabbalistic tradition names the human body *olam katan* – a small cosmos. The body mirrors the cosmos, and each part of the body has spiritual significance. The prophet Ezekiel, alongside his violently misogynistic passages, also tells of a vision in chapter 1 wherein he saw the glory of God as the image of a human being.

The Song of Songs lurks at the heart of the Hebrew Scriptures. It's a joyous celebration of love and physicality.

> As an apple tree among the trees of the wood,
>   so is my beloved among young men.
> With great delight I sat in his shadow,
>   and his fruit was sweet to my taste.

> He brought me to the banqueting house,
>   and his intention towards me was love.
> Sustain me with raisins,
>   refresh me with apples;
>   for I am faint with love.
> O that his left hand were under my head,
>   and that his right hand embraced me!
> (Song of Songs 2.3–6)

It's a wonderful poem. It has influenced many Christian mystics. John of the Cross based his *Spiritual Canticles* on the Song of Songs:

> In the inner cellar, of my Beloved have I drunk,
> And, when I went forth over all this meadow,
> Then knew I naught
> And lost the flock which I followed aforetime.
> There he gave me his breast;
> There he taught me a science most delectable;
> And I gave myself to him, indeed, reserving nothing;
> There I promised him to be his bride.[17]

But St John, along with Christian tradition more widely, denies the obvious eroticism of the poem and treats it as an allegory about the relationship between God and the Church. Origen (c.185–c.253) tries to make the Song of Songs safe:

> This book comes last [in the books attributed to Solomon] so that a person may come to it when his manner of life has been purified ... so that nothing in the metaphors used to describe the love of the Bride for her celestial bridegroom ... may cause him to stumble.[18]

Christianity would not be Christianity without bodies. John's Gospel (1.14) says, 'The Word became flesh and lived among us, and we have seen his glory.' What could be clearer than that? Logos, the pre-existent Word, beyond time and space, beyond infinity, becomes *sarx*, bloody, palpitating flesh in time and space, incarnate in a person in a small province in a backwater of the Roman Empire.

Jesus turns water into wine. He multiplies loaves and fishes. After his resurrection he cooks fish on the beach. In his sermons and teaching he rarely talks about the law or about Judaism; he tells stories about mustard seeds, sowers, vineyards and banquets. He eats with tax collectors and naughty people. He hangs out with people on the margins. Against all the customs of the day he strikes up a friendship with a Samaritan woman. He deliberately undermines the Levitical purity laws which maintained the ritual separation of Jew from Gentile.

Perhaps the last thing I associate with Jesus is shame. He has confidence in his teaching and his life, answering questions with questions, unafraid to challenge the powerful and rich, open to relationships with people from across the spectrum of society. Yet the faith that has the incarnate Christ at its centre has turned shame into a weapon of oppression.

The writings of Paul have been much misunderstood. He does indeed draw a distinction between *sarx* and *pneuma*, but he sees the spirit and the body as one:

> I know a person in Christ who fourteen years ago was caught up to the third heaven – whether in the body or out of the body I do not know; God knows. And I know that such a person – whether in the body or out of the body I do not know; God knows – was caught up into Paradise and heard things that are not to be told, that no mortal is permitted to repeat. (2 Cor. 12.2–4)

The promised transformation is both bodily and spiritual:

> You were taught to put away your former way of life, your old self ... and to be renewed in the spirit of your minds, and to clothe yourselves with the new self, created according to the likeness of God in true righteousness and holiness. (Eph. 4.22–24)

We are created in the image of God and called to be re-created in the image of God, our new selves. As Paul says towards the end of 1 Corinthians:

> Listen, I will tell you a mystery! We will not all die, but we will all be changed, in a moment, in the twinkling of an eye, at the last trumpet ... For this perishable body must put on imperishability, and this mortal body must put on immortality. (1 Cor. 15.51–53)

The ritual at the heart of Christian practice is the Eucharist – Holy Communion – a shared meal during which the body and blood of Christ are, in some mysterious sense, consumed. Battles have been fought and Christendom split over what really happens, but what is beyond doubt is that the bodiliness of Jesus is recalled and recreated. Christianity is an enfleshed faith, and it sings of the body in creation.

We do not *have* bodies, says theologian and writer Isabelle Hamley,[19] we *are* bodies. Exploring the spirit requires us to integrate our bodies and our spirits. There is no distinction. The notion that we can, this side of the grave, free our spirits from our bodies makes no sense – it's like the idea that our minds could be uploaded on to the internet and we could all continue in some parallel world of disembodied intelligence. We couldn't.

To trust the body is liberating. It's exciting. Imagine how it is to be an animal, moving through the world without seeing the body as a burden, without seeing itself as trapped up in a physical envelope that constrains and controls. My friend Sharon Moughtin speaks of her early years of motherhood, when she had had three children within 14 months (two of them were twins) and her life was spent largely on her knees, clearing up after the children. Her moment of light came when someone encouraged her to use the prayer of the body – whenever you find yourself on your knees, that is prayer. 'When I clear a mess off the floor, that becomes prayer.'

The mind and body are inseparable, linked in ways we are only beginning to understand, mysterious and unquantifiable. The human brain, at the last count, has 86 million neurons forming

100 trillion connections with each other and with the body the brain inhabits. So the body keeps count of physical and mental trauma. It is scarred, fragile and easily broken. It is perpetually repairing itself and monitoring its health. Pain can of course be a barrier, building a wall between us and the infinite. Physical and mental illness, hurt and discomfort are real, and are burdensome and hard. There are times when anger and confusion feel like the only possible response to what is happening.

> My God, my God, why have you forsaken me? ...
> I am poured out like water,
>   and all my bones are out of joint;
> my heart is like wax;
>   it is melted within my breast;
> my mouth is dried up like a potsherd,
>   and my tongue sticks to my jaws;
>   you lay me in the dust of death.
> (Ps. 22.1, 14–15)

Making peace with pain and suffering is never easy. But acknowledging the connection between body and spirit is vital to the spiritual journey.

Every body in the world is loved, regardless of its shape or size or colour. There's a joyous video on YouTube – *Good Body*, by Mona Haydar[20] – celebrating that we are all embodied love. Not just embodied, but connected. Sharon speaks of a little-known feature of all bodies, the subcutaneous fascia. The fascia is that thin layer of connective tissue that lies between skin and muscle, the white layer that can sometimes be seen when cutting into a piece of meat. It surrounds every organ in the body, enabling the eye and the hand to be connected and to know, somehow, that they are part of the same body. It's a crucial element of our physical make-up, complementing the central nervous system, giving shape and form to each organ, making sure they don't rub each other to death, bringing unity out of diversity. Without the fascia, bodies could not function; but we only learn about them when something goes wrong.

St Ignatius called his programme of spiritual development the

Spiritual Exercises. It is important to work both on the well-being of our bodies and the health of the spirit. There are ways, simple and straightforward, to nurture both at once. For example: exercising in ways that are consciously spiritual such as yoga; listening attentively to music; being conscious about breath; feeling the endlessly unthanked heart beating in your breast; feeling the sofa's fabric as you sit reading; drinking a glass of water carefully and slowly; sitting in silence and hearing the sounds of your body as it lives and grows and changes and protects and flourishes.

Instead of policing desire, let's embrace desire. Let's understand that desire is a necessary part of love. Human relationships are life-giving. They change the world. They change us. We learn and live and grow through embrace, through physicality, through touch, taste, sound, sight, feeling. Queer or straight, black, brown or white, cisgendered or trans, our physicality matters, in all its beautiful, complex messiness. Of course desire can be horribly misdirected, and we can make of the body an idol, and we can distort love – often because of our own traumatic experiences – so that it becomes destructive to ourselves or those around us. The challenge we all face is to learn how to embrace desire so that it helps us, and the people we love, to flourish. To learn how to let the spirit and the body grow together. To embrace an impure purity that is truly life-giving.

No one is an island. We are, as a species, immersed in one another. We are connected through our bodies. All that communication, all those struggles and disagreements and moments of laughter and meals and conversations and shared smells and shared delights and moments of depth are what enable us to be the people we are. In Part 3 we will think more about the deep unity that underlies everything. For now, it is enough to say that the unity starts with body and spirit. If one thrives, so will the other. But if neither thrive, that way lies death.

6

Exploring nature

The woods on Wimbledon Common were stark and bare, a few crows blackly silhouetted high in the skeletal branches. An overcast and chilly day in December. Mud underfoot, the sound of a chainsaw buzzing through the trees. I crossed the A3 into Richmond Park and walked slowly across the deer-cropped grass. Planes dropped into Heathrow. Twisted, honourable oaks bore witness to the passing of the centuries. I noticed, looked, heard; a deer-fenced copse was alive with birdsong, and high in the overstory I could see long-tailed tits flocking to early winter buds.

I usually try to take a quiet day during Advent, the weeks before Christmas, and that year I decided to walk part of the Capital Ring, a circular walk around the midskirts of London. I set off in the morning and spent the day alone, intentionally aware, watching and listening. Re-forming my relationship with nature. Most of my life is spent surrounded by the noise of sirens and trains grinding over Waterloo viaduct, the only evidence of nature being the churchyard we look after with its superabundance of pigeons and squirrels.

Advent is supposed to be a time of preparation, but December is now a time of consumption, Christmas lights blazing up and down Regent Street and Oxford Street, chocolate liqueur Advent calendars, conspicuous devouring in the name of love and festivity, exhausting the world's resources in the service of capitalism. It felt important to remember the roots that bind us to our natural world.

What Max Weber called disenchantment has had catastrophic effects on our relationship with nature. Capital has become an idol. Monocultures producing abundant cheap food at the cost of animal welfare and biodiversity. The extraction of value from every centimetre of ground, every nook and cranny where minerals can be mined or land exploited. The sea in its death throes, acidifying, warming, fish stocks collapsing. Heartbreaking losses of millions of birds – a 70 per cent drop in bird numbers in the UK in the last 50 years, read that again, *70 per cent* – numberless species going extinct, a maelstrom of plastic in the Pacific Ocean, and of course climate change creeping, no, rushing upon us. Glaciers melting. Seasons confusing. It's all going badly wrong.

Alienation. It would be a mistake to idealize past centuries, or indigenous cultures, but the spiritual cost of this split between nature and culture is huge. I think of the simple beauty of the Christian year, rolling round from Easter, the time of new life, spring springing and sap rising, then Rogationtide when the land was blessed for a good harvest, then Harvest celebrating abundance and the end of the back-breaking labour of bringing in the fruits of the land, and finally the darkness of Advent brightened by the light of Christmas. It's buried, now, in commerce. We have turned nature into an object.

Near the start of the Bible, in the book of Genesis, is the story of the tower of Babel. It follows the story of Noah's flood. The people have multiplied again and conceive a desire to reach beyond God:

> Now the whole earth had one language and the same words. And as they migrated from the east, they came upon a plain in the land of Shinar and settled there. And they said to one another, 'Come, let us make bricks, and burn them thoroughly.' And they had brick for stone, and bitumen for mortar. Then they said, 'Come, let us build ourselves a city, and a tower with its top in the heavens, and let us make a name for ourselves; otherwise we shall be scattered abroad upon the face of the whole earth.' (Gen. 11.1–4)

Can we not build a tower with its top in the heavens, asked the Enlightenment thinkers in the sixteenth and seventeenth centuries? Francis Bacon's scientific method, investigating nature so thoroughly that its mysteries are vanquished; financed by gold from the conquered people of the Americas and by the newly opened trade routes to the East (soon congested with the ships of the European navies and the soldiers of European armies); powered by the rich seams of coal discovered beneath Europe's soil and by the cheap labour of slaves transported to the Americas – the discoveries of the Enlightenment brought about the Industrial Revolution, an all-conquering merging of science and technology in the service of Progress.

Those early peerings down microscope lenses, seeing for the first time the myriad creatures that lurk in a drop of pondwater, have with discovery upon discovery squeezed the sense of awe to the margins. If we know all the parts of a plant, or if we can name all the biological processes that go to make up a butterfly, the mystery is diminished. We may wonder at the colours of a butterfly's wing or the complexity of the relationship between trees, pests and predators, but everything can be rationally explained. It's all come about to fit evolutionary niches.

In which case, what and where and why is God? I picture philosopher René Descartes in the fug of his overheated study in the depths of the Bavarian forest, in 1619, unwilling to write God out completely, believing that the scientific method should also be applied to philosophy, struggling to describe where and how the infinite might rationally connect to the finite.

The soul, he concluded, had its earthly place of residence in the pineal gland, located in the epithalamus in the brain. The body and the mind was a single entity, its workings explicable through experiment and deduction. The function of the soul was to connect matter and spirit, man and God; to create a viaduct for the infinite complexities of faith.

The philosophical descendants of Descartes pushed forward his thought until they thought they had broken free of the constraints of a theistic world-view. Cartesian dualism was pushed towards its logical conclusion.

God, we know enough. We have no need of you. 'Come, let us build ourselves a city, and a tower with its top in the heavens' (Gen. 11.4).

* * *

But this is not the whole story. Beneath the radar, out in the wilds, the old tales of interdependence between God, nature and human beings were finding new champions. Alexander von Humboldt (1769–1859) made many journeys around the world, exploring landscapes new to Europeans, adventuring with electric eels, and developing the notion that the whole of nature, including humanity, is deeply interlinked. The five-volume work *Kosmos*, which he wrote at the end of his life, was his testament to the deep unity of all of creation, under God – he was no atheist:

> It is this necessity of things, this occult but permanent connection, this periodical return in the progress, development of formation, phenomena, and events which constitute 'Nature' submissive to a controlling power.[21]

The great naturalist John Muir – 'Oh, how I wish to be a Humboldt!' – was transformed by his years in the wilderness of Yosemite, and inspired the creation of the first National Parks in the USA.

Tending a flock of sheep in the Sierra foothills through the winter of 1868, he was exhilarated by the unexpected beauty of the California spring. One day, the hills erupting with new plant life, Muir had an experience of the Hollow suddenly overflowing with sunlight 'of an unspeakable richness'; as though 'pouring from a fountain ... You cannot feel yourself,' he wrote later of the incident. 'Presently you lose consciousness of your own separate existence; you blend with the landscape, and become part and parcel of nature.'[22]

'Oh, these vast, calm, measureless mountain days,' he wrote in his journal. 'Days in whose light everything seems equally divine, opening a thousand windows to show us God.'

Pope Francis talked of the mutual responsibility of humankind to ensure that all can benefit from God's creation. In the encyclical *Laudato Si'*, published just before the 2015 COP climate talks in Paris, he introduced a new term – integral ecology. He called for an urgent reform: from taking to sharing, from controlling to caring, from bleeding to feeding.

Our journey into deep spirituality has to pass through the natural world. We are nothing without it. We don't possess nature, we *are* nature. We can't live, spiritually or physically, apart from nature. We flourish as nature flourishes, and we are as fragile as the world around us.

The Sufi tradition within Islam teaches that there are three places where Allah can be perceived: the souls of humanity, the words of the Qur'an, and the natural realm. Rumi, in the Masnavi, writes:

> Time is limited, and the abundant water is flowing away.
> Drink, before you fall to pieces.
> There is a famous conduit, full of the Water of Life:
> draw the Water, in order that verdure may grow up from you.
> We are drinking the water of Khidr
> from the river of the speech of the saints:
> Come, O heedless thirsty man!
> Even if you don't see the water, artfully, like the blind,
> bring the jug to the river and dip it in.[23]

The Qur'an refers often to the relationship between nature and spirit:

> Have those who disbelieved not considered that the heavens and the Earth were a joined entity, and we separated them and made from water every living thing? Then will they not believe? (Qur'an, 21:30)

> Devote yourself single-mindedly to the faith, and thus follow the nature designed by Allah, the nature according to which He has fashioned mankind; there is no altering the creation of Allah. (Qur'an, 30:30)

> It is Allah Who has made for you the earth as a resting place, and the sky as a canopy, and has given you shape and made your shapes beautiful and has provided for you sustenance. (Qur'an, 40:64)

Jesus rarely speaks of the intricacies of faith. His parables are nearly all about the natural world – seeds, vines, sheep. His teachings are rich in natural images: 'Consider the lilies of the field, how they grow; they neither toil nor spin, yet I tell you, Solomon in all his glory was not clothed like one of these' (Matt. 6.28–29). Or think of the intricate relationships so many indigenous peoples have with nature: the aboriginal people in Australia singing the land into being, or Chief Dan George of the Tsleil-Waututh Nation:

> If you talk to the animals they will talk with you and you will know each other. If you do not talk to them you will not know them and what you do not know, you will fear. What one fears, one destroys.[24]

The influential book by Robin Wall Kimmerer, *Braiding Sweetgrass*, celebrates the reciprocal relationship between humans and the rest of the world. She writes of the symbiosis between farmers and the 'holy trinity' of maize, beans and squash – three plants that grow well together, mutually sustaining and providing nourishment for the farmer – and of the relationship between the earth and its inhabitants, which it is not too far-fetched to call love.

* * *

So take a moment to celebrate what my colleague Georgie Bell calls the 'rambunctious queerness' of nature, the astonishing diversity of creation: a thousand different species of banana, four hundred thousand species of beetle.

> If one could conclude as to the nature of the Creator from a study of creation it would appear that God has an inordinate fondness for stars and beetles.[25]

The sheer abundance of reproductive methods, from simple bifurcation through pansexual non-binary regeneration to the chancy but astonishing methods evolved among human beings tells us something profound about spirituality: one size does not fit all, and the overflowing river of spiritual communities reflects the glittering mirror of the cosmos, in its mysterious and often bizarre diversity.

The geologist Teilhard de Chardin, anathemized during his lifetime, is now recognized by many as a visionary:

> I bless you, matter ... in your totality and your true nature. You I acclaim as the inexhaustible potentiality for existence and transformation. I acclaim you as the universal power which brings together and unites. I acclaim you as the divine milieu, charged with creative power. Raise me up then, matter ... until, at long last, it becomes possible for me in perfect chastity to embrace the universe.[26]

He sees the parallels between quantum physics – for example the extraordinary discovery that particles separated by billions of miles, by light years, are mysteriously linked – and the spirit:

> We live in an entangled universe of inseparability where everything is connected to everything else, including God.

He writes of love at the heart of everything:

> Love alone is capable of uniting living beings in such a way as to complete and fulfil them, for it alone takes them and joins them by what is deepest in themselves. Love alone can bring us to the threshold of another universe.

The well-being of the earth is, we now know, incredibly finely balanced. Tiny increases in carbon dioxide in the atmosphere lead to catastrophic weather events. Nudges in an ecosystem can result in collapse. But at the same time, miniscule changes in the genetic sequence bring about the extraordinary resilience which we celebrate and enjoy. Is it an accident that so many poets are drawn to nature and find their inspiration in the world around them? The poet Gerard Manley Hopkins speaks of 'inscape' – the essential 'thingness' that gives identity to every part of the cosmos in the context of the mutability of matter. Inscape is the spiritual reality lying within the material world we can see, touch, hear, feel and smell.

> Glory be to God for dappled things –
> For skies of couple-colour as a brinded cow;
> For rose-moles all in stipple upon trout that swim;
> Fresh-firecoal chestnut-falls; finches' wings;
> Landscape plotted and pieced – fold, fallow, and plough;
> And áll trádes, their gear and tackle and trim.
>
> All things counter, original, spare, strange;
> Whatever is fickle, freckled (who knows how?)
> With swift, slow; sweet, sour; adazzle, dim;
> He fathers-forth whose beauty is past change:
> Praise him.[27]

Celebrate the intricacies of a flower, evolved over eons to be in relationship with a particular insect whose proboscis has developed so specifically that it alone can sup nectar from the scarlet trumpet that bobs in the undergrowth of a tropical forest. Sense the awe-inspiring space which spreads before you as you reach the top of a mountain in the north of Scotland and see the ancient rocks barely clothed in struggling moss, lichen and resurgent Caledonian forest, the rocks all that remain of a mountain range as high as the Himalayas. Wonder at the wonder of the world, silently turning through our tiny galaxy, one of billions that spread out around us, expanding endlessly into a space without time and a time without space. The spiritual urge towards the infinite echoes beyond the edge of the cosmos, but the human spirit can, wonderfully, reach there and find itself reduced to wordless reverence.

And it's good to get your hands dirty. A teaspoon of healthy soil can contain one billion bacteria. Digging into the loam, planting seeds, watching the seedlings sprout, that first flash of green in dark earth, the buds of roses unfurling into golden blooms, scarlet tomatoes ripening in late summer sun; this is what unites creation, body, spirit and nature. The cycle of life and death repeated year after year, spiralling out of the past and into the future, with your grubby fingernails immersed in the present moment. If you don't have access to a garden, a flowerpot will do the trick, or a volunteers' group in your local park. Dig and plant and grow. Tend your own tiny Eden.

You may have to work a little harder to find spiritual moments in the urban jungle. But it's very possible. There are many encouraging stories of natural regeneration in bleak cityscapes. There is a heartwarming video on YouTube about the rewilding of Hackney Marshes.[28] The swift return of field mice and short-tailed voles through recreating habitats and managing the Lea River better is a tale of real love for nature where it might be least expected.

There are always moments of inspiration to be found – early snowdrops appearing in the park, or a bloom you've nourished into being, or the planet Venus glimmering unexpectedly above Waterloo Station, or a peregrine falcon quietly watching over the churchyard – momentary flashes when, however tentatively, you may see the hem of the Lord's robe. My Advent walk through Richmond Park brought me back to my roots in nature. I sat for a time close to a herd of deer munching quietly; the sound of the planes dropped away, the wintery grass took on a beautiful light, and, in the silence, I was touched by the breath of the spirit.

> God is in the midst of the city; it shall not be moved;
> God will help it when the morning dawns. (Ps. 46.5)

7

Exploring lament

In lament, our task is never to convince someone of the brokenness of this world; it is to convince them of the world's worth in the first place. True lament is not born from that trite sentiment that the world is bad but rather from a deep conviction that it is worthy of goodness.[29]

This journey we are on, if it is to be meaningful, can't be comfortable. We've explored the connections between spirit and body, spirit and nature. We've seen how the deep intake of breath fills both body and spirit, and how the whole cosmos is integrated. It's all very awe-inspiring – and so it should be, because creation and nature defy description.

But we also see how fragile everything is. How the cycle of life and death is implacable. The world turns, the universe expands, season follows on from season, plants grow and age and die, animals devour animals, and at the top of the pyramid humanity invades, steals, bombs, exploits, starves, imprisons, shuns, kills, hates. The rich trample on the poor, and everyone kicks everyone. Every schoolroom contains its bullies. Gender-based violence and child abuse are endemic, and the experience of racism, homophobia, transphobia and all the other forms of discrimination can break hearts into a million shards of pain and desolation.

There is so much to lament. The way Black people's bodies have been abused. Stolen, chained up, stuffed into the bottom deck of a noisome ship where shit and piss and puke swirl around the imprisoned bodies, sold into slavery, crushed and crushed again by impossible labour, torn open by rape, broken by the theft of their children, and finally murdered, directly or indirectly, by a lifetime of enslavement. The victims of conflict in Israel/Palestine, subjected to violence as a weapon of war, starved, wounded, broken. The horrors of ethnic violence, genocide, whole peoples stuffed into concentration camps and 're-educated' or killed, or so many massacred that rivers are blocked with the bodies of the dead. The destruction of the natural world – entire mountains mined out of existence.

This is the reality of what Christianity calls sin. It's the desire of humans to scramble up the dung heap, to gain power, to be the king of the castle. Sin is whatever comes between us and the Spirit of love. There is personal sin, my own pride, arrogance or deceitfulness, the ways I wound others – and there is structural sin, the fallout from societal structures and governments and companies that cramp or destroy the lives of the vulnerable or weak.

At the heart of the city it is easy to see the wounds. So many broken people. The homeless men who sleep under the portico in front of my church, each of them damaged in some way: Sid still dealing with the fallout from his tour of duty in Afghanistan; Brian's confidence destroyed by a trauma about which he never speaks; Michael's task being to watch and watch and watch as the doings in the churchyard pass him by. So many broken people coming into church, wanting help, wanting to light a candle, wanting to pray, wanting the rent for a room, wanting hope. So many marches for Palestine, climate justice, Black Lives Matter, the consequences of war and destruction. So many headlines about floods and droughts, hurricanes and heatwaves, wars and rumours of wars, a world going mad, a collective political insanity; the times are out of joint.

In the city it is hard to hide from the pain. I hear the muttering of the person seeing visions, perhaps released from hospital this morning and finding her way to the railway station because that feels like a place of hope. I see the man in a wheelchair, his leg up on a platform, barefoot, overweight, who tells me that he has a bullet in his back from Afghanistan and that he cradled his friend in his arms as life ebbed away. I go and visit Philippa, out of breath and in pain because her kidneys have failed due to the cancer and there is water build-up in her lungs and her legs, and she knows that she has weeks, possibly days, to live.

Where is the spirit? Where is god in all this? What possible sense can we make of the yearning for the infinite when the now is so utterly dysfunctional and the nasty brutish brevity of life seems unavoidable?

I wrote in *Generous Faith* about my own journey, affected by the death of my brother when he was three, before I was born, and by the casual and institutional homophobia with which I have had to contend. The stories of others are much, much harder to hear: the pain and anguish with which terminally ill people too often have to cope; families devastated by the sudden death of a child or a mother in a piece of indiscriminate bombing or starving in a fly-blown refugee camp just across the Sudanese border. What do we do? Do we look, or do we look away, horrified by but trying to evade the raw red agony on display?

We work out our salvation, says St Paul, in fear and trembling. I think of the journey of Abraham with his son Isaac to the mountain of Moriah, where he is to sacrifice his son because he has been told to by Yahweh. This supremely wicked command to Abraham: take your son, your only son (Ishmael is suddenly forgotten) and slay him on an altar at the mountaintop. Danish philosopher Søren Kierkegaard, in *Fear and Trembling*, says that Abraham has to be either a murderer or a man of faith; did he and Isaac and the servant men walk through the desert for three days, Abraham all the time planning how he was to murder his son, or did he believe, hope against hope, that the evil deed he was planning to do would be transformed, somehow, into something that showed the benevolence of the god, Yahweh, whom Abraham worshipped?

We can't make sense of pain or violence or destruction. They are all offences against the cosmos. The problem with evil is that it is all too real, and here, in the city, we see it and feel it and touch it all the time. Social injustice, societal breakdown, the impenetrable barriers between groups. The increase in social isolation, the alarming upsurge in mental health challenges among young people – it's all too real to be ignored.

So am I not being deeply irresponsible, suggesting that you follow me into the wasteland? Or is there another way to understand all this, which would put the pain and the violence in context – not to justify it, never to justify it, but to see how it fits in the jigsaw puzzle that is the intersection of life and death, spirit and matter, which forms the cosmos in which we live? The question is not how but why. Why do we experience pain, loss, grief, alienation, loneliness? Why is the human tendency so often to choose death rather than life, to go for the violent, easy option rather than the loving, difficult option; to seek fulfilment in the shortest term through trampling on the rights and hopes of our fellow human beings and fellow creatures rather than carefully building a different kind of world?

Spiritual direction has been described as a deep dive into the real. An unflinching look at all those multicoloured waltzing pieces, which in a mad devil's dance swirl crazily into chaos. If we are to discover the reality behind the reality we can't avoid the pain. It has its place, it cannot be ignored, it cannot be undone.

In my own life there is too much denial, too much turning away. I move too quickly from despair to hope. Hearing or seeing the sounds and images of destruction, or experiencing the consequences of childhood trauma in those around me – these are too uncomfortable, they make me sad, and I want to cover the world with stardust and pretend that everything is drenched in joy.

But this isn't honest and it doesn't help us understand the spiritual journey. Siddhartha Gautama was insulated by his royal parents from the reality of suffering until he left the palace for the first time, aged 29. He encountered an old man, a diseased man and a decaying corpse. It was his brush with the reality of suffering that transformed his life and drove him towards a life of poverty, and after many years enlightenment and the wisdom that we know as Buddhism.

A comfortable life is a life that presents few challenges. Little is unsettled, the foundations are not shaken, and in complacency lies stasis. 'If it were a choice between Richmond and death,' Virginia Woolf is (wrongly) believed to have said, 'I would choose death.' Unfair on the people of Richmond, but her point is sound.

The journey into the spiritual has the potential to be transformative; to bring us into a new place of unimagined depth. In the New Testament we hear often of the call to repentance, which is usually understood to mean turning away from sin, seeking forgiveness. But the word that is translated so often as repentance has a much richer meaning. The Greek word, *metanoia*, is formed of two roots, *meta*, meaning beyond or new, and *noia*, meaning mind. So we are being called not just to move on from the destructive (which is what I take sinful to mean) habits of our past, but also to move into a new place with a new mind, a new understanding of the world, a radically different place.

The journey calls us into the depths and up to the heights, through the valley of the shadow of death and up mountain ranges to the thin air and bright light of the spirit. In the journey of the hobbits into the caves of Moria, and then Frodo and Samwise's final journey through the forests and into Mordor, Tolkien knew what he was doing when he took them into those dark places where the heart of Frodo's being was challenged and he was sorely tempted to betray everything for the sake of the power the Ring offered him.

To travel along the path asks us not to shrink away from the darkness and woundedness of the world. We can't make sense of the slaughter of the innocents, in Gaza or Ukraine or Sudan or anywhere else, but we cannot look away. We can't make sense of our own will to power, or the traumas and disruptions in our own lives, but we cannot look away. These are the things we put in our backpacks; confronting the pain, remembering the anguish, re-membering the events in our lives or in our world which have torn us apart.

It's easy to feel despair. As the climate changes beyond the most pessimistic predictions of science, as border after border is overrun by autocratic dictators, as the world's leaders seem to become more and more venal, self-serving and corrupt, it's hard to find light in the darkness.

Perhaps that is as it should be. No spirit flourishes in a world that is dishonest. Denial distorts and absolute denial distorts absolutely. If we are to be in deep connection with our siblings, we need to know them, to know their lives, to understand them and to acknowledge them. If our own spirits are to fly, we need to listen to the hurts we have received, to name the pains and injuries that are intrinsic to being a person – to name them, and give them space, so that they can become part of our story and part of the new life we are seeking.

Lament is not despair. Lament is how we give words to the ache we feel at the suffering and sadness in the world. Lament is how our spirits come alongside one another, listening to the heartache and sharing the tears. Lament is the expression of compassion. It is the cry of conviction that life should not be like this. It is opening the gate to a better world.

In the Bhāgavata-purāṇa, (c.800–1000 CE) there is an account of Krishna and his cow-girls. Krishna plays with them in the forest, dances with them and delights them, until suddenly he vanishes, taking only one girl with him. But she, too, experiences the loss of Krishna when he vanishes from her as well, and in the forest she meets the other cow-girls. Desolate, they seek Krishna everywhere, calling out for him, wanting him to return, – until, at last, he relents and returns. Delight ensues again, and the desires of the girls are slaked by Krishna's presence. But, during his time of absence, they are grieving – lamenting – because the closeness to the divine which they were enjoying was suddenly taken away from them.

Lament takes many forms, and arises out of many situations. Within the Jewish tradition, the book of Lamentations in the Hebrew Scriptures cries out in pain at the punishment Yahweh is inflicting upon Jerusalem:

> Is it nothing to you, all you who pass by?
>   Look and see
> if there is any sorrow like my sorrow,
>   which was brought upon me,
> which the LORD inflicted
>   on the day of his fierce anger.
>
> For these things I weep;
>   my eyes flow with tears;
> for a comforter is far from me,
>   one to revive my courage;
> my children are desolate,
>   for the enemy has prevailed. (Lam. 1.12, 16)

The grief the prophet feels is the grief of absence, the grief of betrayal, the grief of promises unfulfilled because of the behaviour of the Israelites. The separation from Krishna, or from Yahweh, the absence of the divine, is what gives rise to the wails of despair rising up from the forest or from the desolate city.

Lament is built into the Christian story. The drama of Holy Week, starting with Jesus' triumphal entry into Jerusalem, takes us into the darkness of despair. Jesus' arrest in the Garden of Gethsemane, his kangaroo trials before Caiaphas and before Pilate, his condemnation, torture and death – all these are remembered during Passiontide. The anguished words of Psalm 22, recalled by Jesus in the Gospel of Mark's account of his death, are repeated over and over again during the liturgies of Holy Week:

> My God, my God, why have you forsaken me?
> Why are you so far from helping me, from the words of my groaning?
> O my God, I cry by day, but you do not answer;
> and by night, but find no rest. (Ps. 22.1–2)

The poetry of Rumi was inspired by the sudden disappearance of his beloved Shams, the one who brought him light, hope and joy, for whom he left everything and with whom he spent many years, infused by divine love, until one evening Shams left their house and, many believe, was murdered by Rumi's younger son.

> Listen to the bamboo flute, how it complains,
> Lamenting his exile:
> Since they separated me from my roots,
> My plaintive notes draw tears from men and women.
> My chest breaks, struggling to release my sighs,
> And express the bouts of longing for my place.
> The one who lives far from his home
> He is always looking forward to the day he returns.
> You can hear my lament for everyone.[30]

When we hear of the slaughter of Palestinians in Gaza or the murder of a child abused to death by her father, or of the exploitation and violence against Black people throughout history, or the relentless destruction of nature by an overweening humanity, we respond with tears and pain. This is a vital response. It is an expression of that quality which is at the heart of our dignity as human beings – compassion. Compassion – literally, feeling with – is the emotion that gives meaning to life. Responding to the cry of the oppressed, grieving when they grieve and lamenting when they lament is a crucial part of the human experience. The psychopath's inability to understand the pain of others is chilling and terrifying, because it takes away something that is at the heart of our identity. I see you, says the greeting in Xhosa, I see you and I hear you.

Jesus looked at the man and loved him (Mark 10.21), we are told, in the story of the rich young man who asks him what he must do to inherit eternal life. The young man goes away sad, for he has many possessions, and Jesus sees how attached he is to his status as a rich man. It is the gaze of love that opens up compassion, and compassion empowers the belief that a better world is possible.

This prayer was prayed by the Revd Munter Isaac, Palestinian priest of the Evangelical Lutheran Christmas Church in Bethlehem, at an ecumenical service in 2023:

> God of love, we lament for all those who have recently lost loved ones. May your Holy Spirit comfort the bereaved families. We call for your mercy, Lord, through lamentation. This land has witnessed so much bloodshed and suffering which has created a vicious cycle of violence. We pray for true transformation, without reverting to a violent status quo, where Palestinians and Israelis are free and equal. Lord, in your mercy, hear our prayer.[31]

Cole Arthur Riley, the African American writer and poet, reflects in her remarkable book *This Here Flesh* on the Black experience in the USA, and how identity is forged through acknowledging the pain:

> Seeing a person or piece of creation trampled should always disrupt something in us. It should always do something to the soul. And when you trace that trampling back across generations and systems and powers, a quiet sorrow is born in you.[32]

So we discern the connection between lament and hope, and see the part that lament plays in the trek towards a deep spirituality.

I am writing this on 28 December, the day when in the Christian year we remember the Holy Innocents – the Feast of the Holy Innocents, no less – when, we are told, all the children aged two or under in Bethlehem were massacred on the orders of King Herod.

> Then was fulfilled what had been spoken through the
>   prophet Jeremiah:
>   A voice was heard in Ramah,
>   wailing and loud lamentation,
>   Rachel weeping for her children;
>   she refused to be consoled, because they are no more.
> (Matt. 1.17–18)

The slaughter of the children is remembered three days after we celebrate the birth of Jesus Christ, in those days supposedly of light and hope between Christmas and Epiphany. It is right to remember them then, because the whole point of the story of the incarnation of God as human is that the world is not as it should be. 'A cold coming we had of it,' say the Magi in T. S. Eliot's poem, 'just the worst time of the year.'[33] Rachel weeps for her children with wailing and loud lamentation, for lament is physical as well as spiritual. The physical act of crying releases salt tears, bitter astringent water speaking of pain and the desert. Weeping is an act of revolution, a way of saying 'No!' to what is happening in the world.

Lament is what happens when we run up against the concrete wall of the inexplicable, when we are brought to a halt by destructive and cruel injustice. Lament is the outworking of the stories of pain and fear that litter the history of the world.

Black spirituality in the USA, expressed with such power and grace by Cole Arthur Riley in *This Here Flesh*, takes the unspeakable brutality of slavery and in acknowledging it turns it into a call for transformation. Jewish spirituality has lament at its heart, in the festival of Yom Kippur, when the book of Lamentations is read, remembering the destruction of the Temple. A spirituality that does not give place to lament is not telling the whole story; it can't be truly authentic. Too many churches, too much Christian spirituality, fails to give place to lament. 'She is at rest,' we say too quickly after a death, or, 'God has a plan and this must be part of it, with prayer you will understand it, there is no need to grieve.'

'It's all in God's good hands,' I said piously to a member of the congregation, to which she replied, 'I'm not quite sure about that. I'm not sure that the people of Gaza or Ukraine think it's all in God's good hands.'

Lament is how complacency is disrupted. Those of us who live in the rich parts of the Global North are insulated in so many ways from the history of displacement and destruction, from the reality of poverty and insecurity, from the present evils of climate-induced horror or the evils of conflict. In hearing the voices of refugees and migrants and the weeping of mothers for their children in the Democratic Republic of Congo or in Yemen, in receiving the anger of the husband whose wife was killed when she was out walking the dog, we can say, 'We are part of this broken world and we do not hide from the harshness of its truths.'

Chine McDonald spoke on lament at St John's, as part of our Exploring Spirit season, but she also spoke on joy. The two, she said, are deeply connected. She spoke of the slaves who, when their work was done, went down to the reservoir to swim and to pray. She spoke of the bodily expression of joy in Pentecostal worship, raised arms, shouts of 'Hallelujah!', giving thanks to God riotously and passionately, lifting hearts, tears of joy erupting from the darkness of loss and enslavement. Joy is an act of revolution too. The Bible speaks of liberation as well as lamentation. The wolf will lie down with the lamb and the child shall play over the hole of the asp, the last shall be first and the first shall be last, God has put down the mighty from their thrones and has exalted the humble and meek.

> You have turned my mourning into dancing;
>   you have taken off my sackcloth
>   and clothed me with joy,
> so that my soul may praise you and not be silent.
>   O LORD my God, I will give thanks to you for ever.
> (Ps. 30.11–12)

The journey from lament to joy is not facile. It needs serious thought, and practice, and engagement. It starts with naming, with hearing, with telling the stories, over and over again. It continues with listening, noticing, receiving those moments of love and justice which bring light into the world.

> Despair does not want to see us reach the promised land. It does not want us to find belonging in our families, or peace down by the reservoir. Our liberation depends on our willingness to resist it. We do this by allowing joy, in whatever form, to be our song.[34]

In this changing and turning world the work is never done, not now, not in the future, not this side of death. And so we continue into the greatest unknown of all, the mystery that is death.

8

Exploring death

Philippa was in her mid-sixties when she was diagnosed with cancer of the oesophagus, at the beginning of 2023. Her children were recently married, and both her grandchildren – Robin and Matilda – were tiny. She had been a member of the congregation at St John's for nearly as long as I had been there, and she was a friend, a mentor, chair of the churchyard committee and a person from whom generosity overflowed. She gave in an astonishing number of ways. To the volunteers in the churchyard, she gave lunches and time and laughter and joy. To a family of boys in church she gave pocket money. To Shanon and me she and her husband David gave the use of their wonderful house in Wales. To her family and to the world she gave time and thought and energy and care.

At first she was angry. Angry that she would not be there to be part of the children's growing up. Angry that her years of retirement were to be snatched away from her. She was angry with God, although she never quite knew whether she believed in God or not – we had many conversations about that – and she was angry with the church, and with me, because I misread the signals and wasn't there for her as she had hoped.

After some gruesome chemotherapy the cancer seemed to go away, and there were cautious hopes at the end of the year. But then there was bad news. Other parts of the body were affected, the lungs, the liver, and it seemed the spread was uncontrollable. After more bouts of chemo and radiotherapy Philippa decided she would have no more treatment. She began to speak of her own death – when I'm not there, it'll be your job to do this, she said to her sister when the children were reaching for their grandmother – and gradually it became clear that the end was approaching.

Her generosity continued. Philippa had hundreds (truly hundreds) of friends, and she made time for all of them. Her family opened their hearts, and in a context that must have been tremendously hard, they welcomed everyone who wanted to see Phil.

As she weakened, her heart seemed to grow. The anger disappeared. She and I had not been able to get back on track after the first diagnosis. We each thought the other didn't really want to meet – I thought that I might, as the vicar, be symbolic of something she didn't want to have to talk about – but her sister managed to unblock the logjam, and in the last few weeks of her life we became close again.

Thank God we did. We were able to meet several times, once for a wonderful supper with Phil and her son John, and once for an enormous croissant brought by her daughter Kitty.

One night, at about 3 a.m., as she was fading, Phil decided in her generosity to set up a WhatsApp group for her husband so that everyone could be told more easily about her death when it came. She named it 'Death Announcement', and added all her friends. She hadn't realized that we would all get messages with that heading. In the morning when we woke up there was shock across the country. Shanon and I spoke, and thought I should try to offer her the last rites – to anoint her. I rushed down on my bike to where she lived and rang the doorbell. David, when he answered, looked surprised, and said that she didn't need anointing right then.

But, a few days later, that moment came, and in a tiny ceremony with Phil and David, I touched her forehead with the oil of chrism blessed by the bishop and prayed for her eternal rest.

Shortly after that, she went into Trinity Hospice in Clapham, and for the last weeks of her life she was surrounded by family, friends and love – love received and love given. Her death, when it came, was quiet and gentle, her husband and family with her. The funeral was attended by 400 people and was a time of wrenching sadness and of great thanksgiving for a life that was an example to all of us.

How do we make sense of death? How do we understand our mortality, and what place does it have on this path? I have written at some length about Philippa – partly in gratitude for the light she brought to the world but also because the manner of her death was profoundly moving.

I'm not sure how many funerals I have taken, but I think it must be over 500. I take fewer now than when I was first ordained; there are fewer old people in Waterloo than there were in Camberwell, and more families opt for a humanist service.

My experience teaches me that religious funerals work well even if the deceased person was not a person of faith, because the liturgy acknowledges the mystery at the heart of life. The words of the funeral service, familiar yet always new, earthy yet always mysterious, touch my heart:

> We have entrusted our sister to God's mercy,
> and we now commit her body to the ground:
> earth to earth, ashes to ashes, dust to dust:
> in sure and certain hope of the resurrection to eternal life
> through our Lord Jesus Christ,
> who will transform our frail bodies
> that they may be conformed to his glorious body,
> who died, was buried, and rose again for us.[35]

Often, during home visits, mourners have looked to me for reassurance that their mother, their wife, their partner, their grandfather is truly at rest, and that their life has in some way not ended. I've affirmed that it does continue – not by pretending to certainty about what happens when we die, but by affirming that it's my belief that we do survive in some inexplicable sense. As St Paul says:

> Listen, I will tell you a mystery! We will not all die, but we will all be changed, in a moment, in the twinkling of an eye, at the last trumpet. For the trumpet will sound, and the dead will be raised imperishable, and we will be changed. For this perishable body must put on imperishability, and this mortal body must put on immortality. (1 Cor. 15.51–53)

Humans seem to be the only creatures who can locate themselves in the context of infinity, and are aware of their impending demise. Some mammals, notably elephants and whales, have ways of acknowledging the death of members of their group. But only humans have devised such elaborate responses to the finality of that moment when breathing stops and consciousness is, apparently, no more. Most religions have death at their heart, dealing with it in a huge variety of ways, from the Hindu belief in the cycle of death and rebirth until the soul is received into Nirvana, to the widespread belief that the ancestors remain with us. In Western Samoa the ancestors are buried in big tombs just outside the front door so they continue to be part of the family.

Fear of death is real. Historically, Christianity foregrounded the threat of hell: those awe-ful frescos in mediaeval churches, with cackling demons waiting by cauldrons for condemned souls, or devils torturing the spirits of the wicked – Dante's circles of hell – the visions of the underworld and paradise in Hieronymus Bosch's picture *The Garden of Earthly Delight*. The threat of eternal damnation also found its way into the Qur'an, replete with depictions of heaven (*Jannah*) and hell (*Jahannam*).

The fear is kept at bay by communal rituals: the joyous funeral processions in the Caribbean; the Irish wake, accompanied by abundant whiskey; the Mexican Day of the Dead. Hallowe'en has become big business, and underlying it is the Festival of All Souls and All Saints, when the souls of the beloved whom we see no longer are remembered at Mass by candles lit in the darkness.

And there is spiritualism, communicating with the dead through occult practices. My grandfather was a senior officer in the Royal Air Force during World War Two. After his retirement he became involved in England's occult subculture, regularly communicating with those who had passed over to the other side. His memorial service at St Clement Danes Church in the Strand was attended by many friends from the occult world. We were told by a medium that Grandfather was present until the address had ended, when he smiled gently and left.

Hasina Zaman came to speak as part of the Exploring Spirit season. She had founded a Muslim funeral directors' service in the East End of London and spoke to us of her experience.

> I do believe in the soul. After ten years of dealing with people who have died, I am very sure that they are still present after death. That's why I was so clear with my staff that they should treat the dead person with respect. Sometimes, I've had help from beyond the grave – if I had a particularly difficult funeral, I would ask for help, and I know I received it.

She spoke of a belief among some Muslims that human existence has five stages: before conception, life in the world, life in the grave, the resurrection, and heaven or hell. She was sure that during the period of life in the grave, the boundaries between life and death are very porous. Grief, she said, is the consequence of love and compassion; we feel grief, we share grief, because our souls are connected. The feeling-with is the outworking of loss. Grief, said Queen Elizabeth II before she died, is the price we pay for love.

Behold, I will tell you a mystery! Is it a joyful mystery or a sorrowful mystery, or both? Death is the opening of the gate to the inconceivable infinite. When God/Yahweh is encountered in the Bible, it's rarely the whole of God which is seen. Moses is shown only the back parts of God. In the Song of Songs the lover is never quite found. Ezekiel in his vision in the Temple sees the hem of the robe of God. Jesus Christ is the earthly manifestation of God in the Trinity because God the creator is far beyond anything that we can fit into our minds.

The infinite, Atman, in Hinduism, cannot be conceived. Nirvana is beyond what can be imagined and the gods in Hindu theology are shards of mirror reflecting the unreflectable.

During the Exploring Spirit session someone spoke about the All Souls service at St John's – the service every 2 November, when we pray for the repose of those who have died.

> I like the idea of the saints and the angels. I like the sense that the host of heaven is there, and that somehow we are going to join it, or they'll join us. My head says this is all rubbish but my heart says there is something inexpressible. Our hearts are expansive. The soul is for ever living, for ever lasting, for ever eternal. It's infinite.

The search for immortality is evident from the earliest human history. There are elaborate graves full of treasures to accompany the dead person to the hereafter, the mummification of corpses, resurrected gods overcoming death.

> Death, be not proud, though some have called thee
> Mighty and dreadful, for thou art not so;
> For those whom thou think'st thou dost overthrow
> Die not, poor Death, nor yet canst thou kill me.[36]

It's a cliché, but clichés contain truth, that Western society has tried to push death to the margins. Apart from natural disasters or epidemics – I was in my twenties when AIDS hit the UK and I lost many friends, and the memory of Covid-19 is still fresh – death now usually happens only to the very old and usually in hospital, privately. The human desire to overcome the stony reality of death is finding a new outlet in the scientific quest for immortality. Dead people don't spend money, and so, apart from the ways in which the market monetizes mortality through funeral rites, death undermines capitalism. Delaying the ageing process is big business. Cyber-storing of brains, the cryonic treatment of bodies, anti-ageing serums and treatments, all of these attempt to cheat death of its power. Why?

Denying death is one of the worst ways to achieve spiritual enlightenment. Death is real; it can't be avoided. The pain that accompanies death is also real, as is the indignity, the loss of identity, the staring into the abyss, the encroaching darkness. Our bodies and our spirits are all that we are, and when we die we are no more. That's reality. The monks who are reputed to have slept in their coffins, or those extraordinarily beautiful still lives ('nature mort' in French) from seventeenth-century Dutch painters, with a skull and a basket of fruit, symbolizing the fleeting nature of life – all these mementos mori are absolutely on point. To deny death is like playing chess but stopping before checkmate is reached.

Christianity has death at the centre – the painful death of Jesus Christ, after he was betrayed, crowned with thorns, mocked, spat at and publicly crucified. Good Friday is a time of deep sadness, and Holy Saturday, the day when Christ is dead, even more so. The Word became flesh and dwelt among us, full of grace and truth – even to the point of embracing mortality. Jesus could have turned his face away from Jerusalem, but he didn't. Through his willingness to enter into ephemeral life, we created beings are able to share in divinity.

By acknowledging the reality of death, the focus turns to the here and now. I often speak to people who have been brought up to think that there is a real risk that they may go to hell. It's a hard thing to unlearn; the fear runs very deep. But I am sure that such condemnation is incompatible with belief in a god who is love. A spirituality that nourishes enables us to live well, now, in the days and months and years of this life rather than living in fear of the next.

I asked Hasina what we should do to prepare for our deaths.

> Before, my response to that question was very legal – you should talk to your kids, make a will, make sure everything is in order. But now I would say, just live your best life. However you're going to die you're going to die. If you want to do something go for it. Last night, I met this lady who told me her ambition was to be a tailor in Saville Row. She's sticking at it because it's her love. If she's following her love she is feeding her soul. Don't limit yourself. Just do it.

I recall the sentences I have said so many times at the start of funerals as I lead the coffin into church or into the chapel:

> In the midst of life we are in death;
> to whom can we turn for help,
> but to you, Lord?[37]

The spiral of existence relies on death to bring about new life. Soil is made up of decaying plants and leaves and animals, and a rich soil is full of death, providing food for a billion bacteria in every spoonful. Reincarnation recognizes this; we humans are constantly relaunched into the cycle of life, just as roses fade and fall and provide soil for new roses to sprout. Islam and

Christianity hold the vision of a final resurrection for the whole of creation, and Judaism looks towards the coming of the Messiah for fulfilment. Those outbursts of joy which complete the great symphonies of Beethoven or Bruckner speak of the radiance of the time to come – a time inconceivable and yet full of hope. 'For we brought nothing into this world, and we can take nothing out,' reads the first letter of Timothy; true enough, but here is the whole passage:

> Of course, there is great gain in godliness combined with contentment; for we brought nothing into the world, so that we can take nothing out of it; but if we have food and clothing, we will be content with these. But those who want to be rich fall into temptation and are trapped by many senseless and harmful desires that plunge people into ruin and destruction. For the love of money is a root of all kinds of evil, and in their eagerness to be rich some have wandered away from the faith and pierced themselves with many pains.
> But as for you, [child] of God, shun all this; pursue righteousness, godliness, faith, love, endurance, gentleness. (1 Tim. 6.6–11)

I come back to Philippa, and the possibility of a good death. I add my grandfather's conviction that we make our own afterlife, and Hasina's firm belief that the soul continues, and the persistent belief throughout history that for humanity death is not the end. Our lives after death are defined by the love we gave and the love we are willing to receive in this life. We deprive death of its power by living fully in the present, by allowing our experience of the everyday to be the thing that gives us life, by not fearing death but celebrating life, by feeding our spirits with spiritual food and our physical bodies with physical food. That's how we receive eternal life – by bringing infinity into the immediate, discovering the eternal now.

There are times in my life when I have had a brush with death – a car accident in Syria, being caught in an ocean current in Western Samoa, an overdose of class A drugs in Walworth. Each of them have driven home to me how vital it is to live in the present, with gratitude and generosity. To relish the moments of love and deliciousness, to inhabit the moments of fear and depression – not to deny the challenges but to make sure that I learn from them and try to live better, more carefully, more compassionately.

In the midst of life we are in death. It reminds me of the time when, after a two-day walk through the rainforest in Borneo, Shanon and I arrived at a great waterfall, the river crashing into a big pool and then thundering again over the edge into another. Between the falls, the pool was very swimmable; and so we swam, aware of the risks but loving the cool of the water after the heat of the jungle. We live in the moment between the cascade into new life and the cataract of death; in this moment, the here and now, we learn to swim, and we learn to play.

Death, be not proud.

9

Exploring justice

For the eleventh or twelfth time we assembled in a church in central London. There were about 50 of us, wearing woolly hats and keffiyehs (Palestinian scarves) and coats and gloves, for it was cold outside. We left our banners at the back of church: Blessed are the Peacemakers; Ceasefire Now; Stop the Genocide; End Apartheid; Christians for Palestine. I met up with Deborah, Laych and Sister Maureen, and together with the other members of Christians for Palestine we prayed for the victims of the events on 7 October 2023 and the victims of the bombings and killings since.

For the eleventh or twelfth time we left the church to join the march. We waited at the side of the road until we saw the Jewish Solidarity for Palestine bloc approaching. Once they had gone past, we fell in behind them, along Piccadilly and down Haymarket, into Trafalgar Square and on to Parliament Square.

The demonstration was good natured, as usual. I saw people I see on most marches, for this was the eleventh or twelfth time, and we had begun to know each other. The prayers were becoming familiar, and we had sung many times the great plea for peace:

Let it flow through me,
Let it flow through me,
Let the mighty power of God
Flow out through me.[38]

When I woke up that Saturday morning I asked myself, what on earth is the point of going on another march? What possible difference can it make? The bombing goes on and thousands of people are dying and there is no sign of a ceasefire. Are we making any difference at all?

I knew the answer. I knew that I was going to march, because really I had no choice. It felt like one small thing which I could do to acknowledge the cataclysm that after the decades-long struggle had engulfed the people of Gaza. I could be a tiny part of the fifty or eighty thousand people who would gather in central London to show the Palestinians that they are not forgotten. I knew that the marches around the world were seen, and heard, and they gave courage to the people who were scrabbling through rubble for survivors or trying to give medical aid to women and children whose legs had been blown off or were suffering from cholera because of insanitary water. To march was my tiny act for peace; and alongside the people of Palestine and Israel I remembered so many other places where people are suffering because of war or suppression – Ukraine, the Democratic Republic of Congo, Sudan, Yemen, Myanmar, the Uighurs in the 'political re-education camps' in western China ...

I ended the previous chapter suggesting that in the here and now we learn to swim and to play. Perhaps that word, 'play', was jarring. How dare I speak of play in a world of so much suffering? Am I not belittling the human struggle?

No. Play is vital for spiritual well-being. A good life is a life of human dignity, a life where we can laugh and weep, dance and march, and work together against the structures of power and violence that cause such terrible damage. A good life is a life of abundance in a world where the dignity and worth of every person is recognized and celebrated. A good life is a life where play is deadly serious, because play is part of the spectrum of actions that bring change.

Ivan Illich said this:

> One aspect of modernity was the loss of gratuity ... With the Enlightenment, philosophers largely stopped speaking about ethics and morals as the search for the good and increasingly spoke instead about the valuable ... The valuable always implies some relationship to effectiveness, to efficiency, therefore to device, to tool, to purpose. It has become very difficult

at the end of the modern time to imagine actions which are good and beautiful without being in any way purposeful.[39]

Illich refers often to the parable of the good Samaritan – the story about a Jewish man beaten and left for dead in the ditch. A priest and a lawyer pass by on the other side, but a Samaritan (the Samaritans had little to do with Jews) picks him up, bandages his wounds and takes him to an inn where he can recover. The Samaritan was the neighbour of the man who was beaten up. Illich sees the life and teachings of Jesus as 'a glorious revelation of the freedom to turn in love towards the other, whoever it may be'.[40]

Dignity, freedom, love, justice. If all humans are made 'in the image of God', as we are told in that great poem of creation that opens the book of Genesis, then all humans should be treated with the dignity and respect with which we approach God. If god is goodness and love absolutely and without remainder then each of us is commanded to treat those around us and the created order with goodness and love. It's not a question of transactional value – of saying that I will behave well towards you so that you may, at some stage in the future, behave well towards me. It's a vision of liberation. We have the freedom to choose to turn in love towards the other, whoever the other may be.

But we live in a broken world, where the powerful stamp on the necks of the vulnerable, where slavery, colonialism and capitalism have resulted in merciless exploitation of races, peoples and the planet. The reality of suffering and of pain is acknowledged by the Buddha's insight that existence is dukkha, by Jewish prophets' anguish at the way the rich and powerful exploit the widow and the orphan, by the Qur'an's emphasis on *'adl* (justice) and *mizan* (balance), as imperative for all believers. The Bhagavad Gita, part of the great epic Mahabharata, is the god Krishna's call for justice in the face of the warrior Arjuna's doubts:

Arjuna, whenever righteousness is on the decline, unrighteousness is in the ascendant, then I am reincarnated. For the protection of the virtuous, for the extirpation of the evil-doers, and for establishing Dharma [righteousness] on a firm footing, I am born from age to age.[41]

The call to work for a juster, fairer world is at the heart of the Christian gospel. Here is the beginning of Jesus' ministry, recounted in the Gospel of Luke:

> When [Jesus] came to Nazareth, where he had been brought up, he went to the synagogue on the sabbath day, as was his custom. He stood up to read, and the scroll of the prophet Isaiah was given to him. He unrolled the scroll and found the place where it was written:
> 'The Spirit of the Lord is upon me,
>   because he has anointed me to bring good news to
>   the poor.
> He has sent me to proclaim release to the captives
>   and recovery of sight to the blind, to let the oppressed
>   go free,
> to proclaim the year of the Lord's favour.' (Luke 4.16–19)

The belief that the reign of God will not come without the liberation of the oppressed inspired liberation theologians in the twentieth century, especially in Latin America, subject at that time to the rule of fascist dictators. The Sabeel Ecumenical Liberation Theology Centre was founded in the 1940s by the Revd Naim Ateek. Samuel Munayer, a young Palestinian theologian, spoke from Jerusalem at a gathering in London in December 2024:

> The Christmas story is illuminated by the situation of Palestine ... The incarnation of Christ happened amidst a Roman occupation and massacres where King Herod wanted to kill the babies, using his earthly means in order to assert his true sovereignty, and now you have mothers and fathers who are fleeing, trying to give birth ... so Palestine and Christmas are interpreting one another. If we follow the ways of empire in trying to discern where Jesus is, we might end up in Herod's palace rather than the manger, where Jesus was born. God's

incarnation to the earth was not one which was neutral: God identified with the oppressed and fought for liberation. God has the last word, because God was incarnated as an oppressed person, and therefore that gives us hope.[42]

* * *

Martin Luther King was part of a humbling tradition of Black empowerment in the face of slavery and the Jim Crow legislation, which replaced slavery after abolition. He grew up in a world where lynchings were common. White families would attend them with a picnic and send postcards of the murder to their friends afterwards – 'This is the barbecue we had last night. Your son, Joe.'

In the face of such entrenched evil, generations of women and men developed a theology of resistance, which nurtured King and his wife, Coretta Scott King, and many others.

Power without love is reckless and abusive, and love without power is sentimental and anaemic. Power at its best is love implementing the demands of justice, and justice at its best is power correcting everything that stands against love.[43]

African American churches emerged at the beginning of the nineteenth century, embodying the resistance of Negro spirituals. They underpinned the work of women such as Harriet Tubman, Maria Stewart and Sojourner Truth, each witnessing to human dignity in the face of unconscionable oppression.

In the classic novel *Beloved*, by Toni Morrison, the grandmother Baby Suggs had been an itinerant preacher in the Deep South. She used to gather her people in the Clearing, deep in the woods, and there she told the children to laugh, the men to dance and the women to weep until all were dancing, laughing and weeping together. When all were exhausted, and lying about the Clearing damp and gasping for breath, Baby Suggs, 'holy, offered up to them her great big heart'.

She did not tell them they were sinners and should repent. She did not tell them that they were the meek, bound for glory only after death. She told them to love; love their flesh, love their broken bodies, love their feet that need rest and their unnoosed necks and the dark, dark liver –

> And the beat and beating heart, love that too. More than eyes or feet. More than lungs that have yet to draw free air. More than your life-holding womb and your life-giving private parts, hear me now, love your heart. For this is the prize.[44]

Spirit plus love makes justice. Spirit plus justice makes love. Love plus justice makes spirit. Naming and overcoming the insidious power of deception, hypocrisy, fear and hate is not easy. It is a struggle. But it is a struggle rooted in the teaching and life of Jesus, manifested in his encounter with the Samaritan woman at the well in the Gospel of John. The woman, an outcast, is at the well in the heat of the day away from those who have shunned her. Jesus asks her for a cup of water, and she is drawn into conversation with him. They create a relationship, shocking to his disciples when they return from their errands in town, but transformative for her. When Jesus takes his leave of her she rushes back to the town from which she has been rejected, saying, delightedly, 'Come and see a man who told me everything I have ever done!' (John 4.29).

Howard Thurman grew up alongside Martin Luther King who is reputed to have carried Thurman's book *Jesus and the Disinherited* with him wherever he went. He was a preacher and teacher who grounded his resistance to racial discrimination on a clear-sighted analysis of the deception, hypocrisy, fear and hate that underly oppression and distort both the oppressor and the oppressed.

> For the privileged and the underprivileged alike, if the individual puts at the disposal of the Spirit the needful dedication and discipline, he can live effectively in the chaos of the present the high destiny of a son of God.[45]

Black spiritual and political empowerment intersects with one of the most urgent issues of our time – climate disruption. In 2014,

I founded Faith for the Climate, a charity that brings together people from many faith traditions to work on climate change and climate justice. Faith for the Climate works with Buddhists, Brahma Kumaris, Christians, Hindus, Quakers, Jews, Muslims, Sikhs, pagans – anyone who identifies with a faith tradition and is actively responding to the climate crisis. We have, together, raised our voices to call for a just transition to a fossil-fuel-free economy. We have marched, sung, had interfaith picnics as part of the Great Big Green Week, demonstrated and met with senior policy-makers and politicians. Faith for the Climate became the secretariat for faith groups in the UK that wanted to advocate more ambitiously for climate justice at the COP26 talks in Glasgow in 2021. Since then we have developed a series of workshops with young people who recognize the injustice that those who have done the least to cause climate change are suffering most.

We are inspired by the work of Black activists in the UK and abroad. Vanessa Nakate, in Uganda, and Mikaela Loach in the UK are just two of the many passionate and articulate young people from the Global Majority working on climate today. I was honoured to interview Mikaela in Southwark Cathedral in 2024; her commitment to justice and to the flourishing of people and planet are an inspiration to thousands. She connects spirituality with justice in her book *It's Not That Radical*:

> When we are transformed, we transform the world around us. Unlike caterpillars who only get to do their transformation once, we get to do it over and over. Each time is easier and more beautiful than the last – but only if we keep our ears open to listen and our hearts open to be moved.[46]

The climate crisis has been described as a wicked issue, because its ramifications reach into every part of human and natural life. Two magisterial documents have been produced that place responsibility for the crisis firmly at the feet of consumerism. *Laudato Si'* was startling in its reach and in its uncompromising call – particularly to the West – to take a different path.

The ecological crisis is a summons to profound interior conversion. It must be said that some committed and prayerful Christians, with the excuse of realism and pragmatism, tend to ridicule expressions of concern for the environment. Others are passive; they choose not to change their habits and thus become inconsistent. So what they all need is an 'ecological conversion', whereby the effects of their encounter with Jesus Christ become evident in their relationship with the world around them.[47]

Al-Mizan is the definitive Muslim response to the climate crisis, published in 2024, partly inspired by *Laudato Si'*. *Mizan* is the Arabic word for balance, one of the principles of Islamic justice. An unjust world is a world that is out of balance, where nature cannot thrive, where the poor have their sustenance taken away from them. Cosmic balance is linked in the Qur'an to equity, fairness and justice.

> We sent our messengers with clear signs. And We sent down the Book and the Balance with them so that humankind might establish fairness. (Qur'an 57:25).

> And the Earth, We have spread it out, and cast in it mountains standing firm, and grown in it all things in balance. And We have provided in it sustenance for you and for those whom you do not support. (Qur'an 15:19–20)

> And the sky, He (God) raised it and He set up the balance so that you may not exceed the balance. And the Earth He has spread out for all living creatures. Weigh with justice and do not fall short in the balance. (Qur'an 55:7–10)[48]

* * *

I grieve when I see that one part of creation is unable to flourish, whether it is the rainforests of Borneo, or Black people enslaved in the British Empire or in the USA, or vulnerable children damaged by abuse, or trans people vilified for wanting to be their true selves. During a discussion about inclusion in the Church of England, a bishop asked me, crossly, 'Since when has diversity been a virtue?' To which I replied, 'Um, since the dawn of creation?'

The writers of Genesis understood the miracle of creation, its complexity and interdependence; all the species of animals are called into the ark, and the ark must be huge in order to contain them all.

Nature is indeed rambunctiously, joyfully queer. Nothing is normal but everything coheres. There is no 'normal' animal; aardvarks are no more standard than amoebas, and tigers than tortoises. There is no 'normal' plant; yews, yuccas and yams have wildly different biological make-ups, and the range of colours in the world of plants and animals could hardly be more wonderful. There is no 'normal' human either. Black people are not more normal than Brown, men than women, lesbian or gay than heterosexual. Nature functions because everything has found or is finding its niche.

The prophet Muhammad said, in what is known as his Farewell Sermon:

All of you descend from Adam and Adam was made of earth. There is no superiority for an Arab over a non-Arab nor for a non-Arab over an Arab, neither for a white man over a black man nor a black over a white man except the superiority gained through consciousness of God. Indeed the noblest among you is the one who is most deeply conscious of God.[49]

Diversity is holy and spiritual. Queerness is holy and spiritual. The diversity of humanity has evolved in response to the diversity of geography and geology and genes, because of the difference in sunlight between the equator and the poles, because of the difference in diet between rainforest and tundra. It is all amazing, and to live in a just world is to live in a world that celebrates difference. The levelling out of nature by monocultural capitalism or the rejection of different colour skins or cultures by nationalistic politicians are precisely equivalent, for both are inimical to life.

If the world is wounded, we are wounded. This is what our

spirits lament. This is why we call for justice. As Rowan Williams says:

> Living in or according to 'spirit' (and it is seldom clear whether this means simply and directly the Spirit of God or whether it includes ourselves as 'spiritual') is a designation of the entire set of our human relations, to God and each other and our environment.[50]

***

Not everyone is called to act in the same way. Martin Gainsborough, Bishop of Kingston, came to St John's as part of Exploring Spirit to speak about politics:

> All of us will find ourselves in different places on different issues. A bishop is called to amplify voices on the margins. For other people, the vocation might be to be on the barricades, to be an activist. In my recent visit to the Holy Land, I saw the injustices the Palestinians are experiencing, but I was also moved profoundly by meeting Israeli Jews. That felt important to me. So my question is, what are we individually called to do?

For each of us, the answer is different. One person is moved in their guts by the plight of homeless people on the streets of their city. Another by the refugees trying to get to a safe country, resorting to the dangers of a tiny boat on a storm-tossed English Channel. Another by the fast disappearing island nations in the South Pacific, and another by the harm done to disabled people by the lack of good access. Each of us brings our skills and our compassion, our hope and our vision, working in specific ways on specific tasks, because no one person can do everything.

Not all are guilty, said the Polish American Rabbi Heschel, but all are responsible. The injustices we see are injustices that have built up over centuries and might take centuries to be resolved. No matter. We do what we can. What is clear is that, as Bishop Martin said, 'What is antithetical is to be indifferent, and Christianity does not allow you to be indifferent.'

We are entangled in relationships of power, caught up in oppressive power structures. Of course we connive, at times, and collude, at times, because life is often more comfortable if we don't make waves, and it can be exhausting continually to protest. But dead fish do not swim against the current. A spirituality rooted in contemplation can't flourish without action, just as a life of active engagement can't flourish without a healthy spirituality.

So when I wake on a day when there is a march for Palestine in London, I march. Not because I think everyone should march – although a few more people would be welcome. Not because I think the Palestinian situation is the only one that deserves attention; how could I possibly think that? But there is a particular tragedy about the tearing apart of communities and cultures in what is still known as the Holy Land, and about the terrible history in which Christianity and empire have played a leading role in bringing us to this point. These few square kilometres of fertile land, once flowing with milk and honey, now potentially capable of producing abundant olives and oranges, the cradle of the Abrahamic faiths, should be a model for the world of how cultures and people can live together in love and respect, and instead it's being ripped apart.

As I march I feel a strange combination of lament and joy. Lament at the desperation and destruction. And joy, because among the thousands on the streets, the drumming and the singing, the banners and the brightness, a community emerges. Justice is a communal act. We are all in complex webs of communities of families, friends, work, interest, passions, faith and politics. A spider's web, drenched in dew and caught in the morning's sunlight, is a thing of great beauty. Pull one strand, though, and the whole web trembles. It is the beauty and fragility of community, whether activists on the street or worshippers in the mosque or temple, which brings spirituality out of the realms of theory and into the arena of practical action. As Rabbi Hillel said in the first century BCE:

If not you, then who? And if not now, then when?[51]

10

Exploring light

At dawn on the first day of the week I crawl out of bed and make my way to the forecourt of the darkened church. We gather around a brazier, the clergy and servers wearing white robes, a golden stole to mark Easter, little unlit candles in our hands, a few people shivering in the early cold. A night bus rumbles past. The deacon is carrying a big white candle, nearly a metre long. We say these ancient words:

> Eternal God,
> who made this most holy night
> to shine with the brightness of your one true light:
> set us aflame with the fire of your love,
> and bring us to the radiance of your heavenly glory;
> through Jesus Christ our Lord.
> **Amen.**[52]

I touch a lit taper to the brazier. Fire licks through the paper and wood, flames glimmering against the darkness of Waterloo. I take the candle and, using the taper, light the wick. A tiny flame shines out and Georgia, who is deacon today, leads us into the blackness of the church. At the top of the steps she stops, lifts high the candle, and sings:

> 'The Light of Christ!'
> The congregation responds:
> 'Thanks be to God!'[53]

The dawn Mass is one of the pinnacles of the church's year. I love the moment when the candle is borne into the empty and lightless space of the nave, and the candlelight, so gentle, warms the whole place. It is called the paschal candle, for Easter. It is placed in a special candlestick, dark blue ceramic, made for St John's by Royal Doulton in the nineteenth century. From it, we take the light and light our small candles, and then Georgia begins to sing the ancient words:

> Rejoice, heavenly powers! Sing, choirs of angels!
> Rejoice all creation around God's throne!
> Jesus Christ our Lord is risen! ...
> Grant that this Easter Candle may make our darkness light.
> For Christ the morning star has risen in glory;
> Christ is risen from the dead and his flame of love still burns
>   within us![54]

Light and spirit are deeply intertwined. Light is at the heart of many religious traditions. In the Qur'an, the prophet Muhammad is described as light – *noor* – and Allah thus:

> God is the Light of the heavens and earth. His Light is like this: there is a niche, and in it a lamp, the lamp inside a glass, a glass like a glittering star, fuelled from a blessed olive tree from neither east nor west, whose oil almost gives light even when no fire touches it- light upon light- God guides whoever He will to his Light; God draws such comparisons for people; God has full knowledge of everything.[55]

In the reports of the Prophet's teaching, words and actions known as the Hadith, Ibn Abbas reported:

> He [Ibn Abbas] spent the night with the Messenger of Allah, peace and blessings be upon him, and he woke up. The Prophet cleansed his teeth, performed ablution, the call to prayer was announced, and he went out for the prayer while he was saying,
> 'O Allah, place light in my heart and light on my tongue. Place light in my hearing and light in my seeing. Place light behind me and light in front of me. Place light above me and light below me. O Allah, grant me light!'[56]

In the Hindu Scriptures, light (*jyoti*, or *prakash*) is life itself. The Gayatri Mantra is an invocation to the God of light, to illuminate the world with the wisdom of understanding. It has been translated many times, for example by the American poet Ravi Shankar:

> Oh manifest and unmanifest,
>   wave and ray of breath,
> red lotus of insight,
>   transfix us from eye to navel
> to throat, under a canopy of stars,
>   spring from soil in an unbroken
> arc of light that we might
>   immerse ourselves until lit
> from within like the sun itself.[57]

Think of Stonehenge, miraculously constructed for the moment of sunrise at the summer solstice. Think of the opening of the book of Genesis:

> In the beginning when God created the heavens and the earth, the earth was a formless void and darkness covered the face of the deep, while a wind [*ruach*] from God swept over the face of the waters. Then God said, 'Let there be light'; and there was light. (Gen. 1.1–3)

Why is light such a powerful spiritual metaphor? It starts with the cosmos. The celestial bodies which give light – the stars – are what give life to the universe. Light is a by-product of the nuclear processes that make stars and galaxies what they are. There would be no life without light. Light – in particular ultraviolet light – is the essential element of photosynthesis, by which the first oxygen-producing organisms emerged, leading to plants, animals and ultimately to you and me.

Without sunlight, we die. With sunlight – not too much, but enough – we and the biosphere flourish. Light enables us to see the world around us so that we can plant plants and rear animals and produce food and art and communities and beautiful things.

It brings about enlightenment. That's the irony behind the dominant narrative of the Enlightenment in Europe and America, speaking of a disenchanted world instead of one imbued with light.

Light is related to but not the same as electricity. Electricity is the flow of charged particles, light is the vibration of charged particles. The greater the charge, the brighter the light. Light can create electricity through the photo-electric process. Light is essential for communication via symbols such as letters and pictures and along fibre-optic cables. Light is at the heart of spiritual experience; meditative practices often focus on a mystical light, and near-death experiences speak of a tunnel leading to a bright and effulgent light.

For light to get through there must be transparency. Or it must be reflected. It must be given away. Illumination is reflected light. A red surface is a surface that keeps all the colours except red, which it gives back. White light is light that has been reflected in its entirety.

It can't be stored, unlike electricity. Now you see it, now you don't. Close the door and the light is gone. We can't build warehouses and fill them with light; the only thing we can do with it is receive it as a gift and pass it on. Light is what is given away; if you try to hold it, it vanishes. It's like love. Love must be given away; to hold on to love kills it. Light is the life-force; it is the manifestation of love in the cosmos. That's why light and love and spirituality are so entwined.

Light is the opposite of darkness. Darkness is the absence of light. Darkness is shade – the dark side of the moon – or it is where there is no source of light. Darkness is feared because it is cold and unforgiving and alien and frightening. Darkness is the place where the devil lurks. Darkness is the place of lament, of pain, of suffering. We speak of the black dogs of depression and of being locked into black despair. The land of Mordor is a dark place. The caves of the underworld are lightless and contain lurking creatures as black as pitch. We enter into the darkness of death. Dungeons are dark, and the dark night of the soul is, in common understanding, a place of despair.

So darkness must be vanquished by light. As we read in the

opening of the Gospel of John (1.5): 'The light shines in the darkness, and the darkness did not overcome it.'

But must it? Are darkness and light really such binary opposites, or is there something more profound going on? Is there a sense in which darkness and light are co-inherent, and perhaps darkness is as essential as light on the spiritual path?

Not every spiritual tradition fears the darkness. Shiva, one of the top gods in the Hindu pantheon, is both destroyer and creator. He represents the truth that death is necessary for the creation of new life. In Chinese cosmology, in the yin/yang symbol, there is in darkness a spark of light, there is in light a spark of darkness. Darkness is where seeds germinate and take root. The darkness of the womb or the egg is where new life is formed, and our eyes, concave as they are, are dark so that they can receive the light outside. Darkness is the place of sleep for most creatures, and of dreams for people and, possibly, creatures, though we cannot be certain of this. We close our eyes to seek release from stress and overstimulation. We close our eyes in prayer or meditation.

Darkness is the medium through which light travels. Darkness is how we see the stars in the cosmos. To be sure, before humanity understood that the moon can encompass the sun, it was a fearful thing when the sun was eclipsed and darkness covered the earth. It is a fearful thing that black holes are infinitely dense, so much so that they absorb and devour not only light but everything around them. It is a fearful thing to walk through a wood at night and not know what caused the crack of a branch in the shadowy undergrowth. Think of skeletal trees against a grey sky, leaves all gone, tangled crows' nests clinging to the bare branches, a frightful image, those black birds symbolizing curses and misfortune.

But it is also a wonderful thing to be able to close our eyes in sleep and to dream. It is a wonderful thing for a seed to land in dark soil and burrow in to find the minerals and elements it needs to put out roots and shoots and create bright flowers and sweet fruits.

It is also, more challengingly, a wonderful thing to find the courage to face our fear. Just as the darkness of loam is essential for the creation of new plant life, so facing the darkness is essential for our own spiritual journeys.

I have grown as a person not so much in the easy, relaxed and joyful times but more in the times when I have been forced to dig into the dark depths of my resourcefulness, to discover how much I am able to cope with, how much reaching out to friends and community brings help and relief. Like cross-country runners, we need to go through the moments when we feel we can't make it, in order to discover that we can. In moments of need and despair we can reach out our hands to find the strength and comfort of strangers and people we love and who love us. It is when we feel most afraid that we send out those unexpected prayers, or when we turn to the groundbass of god, the spiritual heart of the universe, to ask for help and healing.

Artists and musicians understand this. Monet's oil paintings of the River Thames are the artist's obsessive attempts to capture the transient light of the London fogs of the time – sulphuric air smirching the brightness, causing daytime darkness and night-time luminescence. One of my favourite composers is Franz Schubert, a man whose music slides perpetually from major to minor and back to major again. Some of his greatest music is the bleakest – the song cycle Winterreise, or the slow movement of the C-major string quartet. Time and time again he mingles hope and despair, bringing light out of a darkness he depicts with deep and arresting accuracy.

The entangling of light and dark is at the heart of one of the greatest psalms. In Psalm 139, the poet displays her utter conviction that darkness and light are two sides of the same coin; both are essential to life.

> If I take the wings of the morning,
>   and settle at the farthest limits of the sea,
> even there your hand shall lead me,
>   and your right hand shall hold me fast.
> If I say, 'Surely the darkness shall cover me,
>   and the light around me become night',
> even the darkness is not dark to you;
>   the night is as bright as the day,
>   for darkness is as light to you.

For it was you who formed my inward parts;
> you knit me together in my mother's womb.
I praise you, for I am fearfully and wonderfully made.
> Wonderful are your works;
that I know very well.
> My frame was not hidden from you,
when I was being made in secret
> > intricately woven in the depths of the earth. (Ps. 139.9–15)

St John of the Cross wrote in the sixteenth century of the dark night of the soul. John had more than his share of challenges – he was locked in a cupboard for nine months by his fellow monks and escaped in the end by tying his bedsheets together. He was in an often-fiery relationship with his friend and co-reformer, St Teresa of Avila. He wrote a poem and commentaries, which have become essential reading in the spiritual canon.

The Dark Night of the Soul speaks of the time when all seems lost, and yet it is the time most blessed.

> On a dark night,
> Kindled in love with yearnings – oh, happy chance! –
> I went forth without being observed,
> My house being now at rest.
>
> In darkness and secure,
> By the secret ladder, disguised – oh, happy chance! –
> In darkness and in concealment,
> My house being now at rest.
>
> In the happy night,
> In secret, when none saw me,
> Nor I beheld aught,
> Without light or guide, save that which burned in my heart.
>
> This light guided me
> More surely than the light of noonday
> To the place where he (well I knew who!) was awaiting me –
> A place where none appeared.

Oh, night that guided me,
Oh, night more lovely than the dawn,
Oh, night that joined Beloved with Lover,
Lover transformed in the Beloved!

Upon my flowery breast,
Kept wholly for himself alone,
There he stayed sleeping, and I caressed him,
And the fanning of the cedars made a breeze.

The breeze blew from the turret
As I parted his locks;
With his gentle hand he wounded my neck
And caused all my senses to be suspended.

I remained, lost in oblivion;
My face I reclined on the Beloved.
All ceased and I abandoned myself,
Leaving my cares forgotten among the lilies.[58]

According to John of the Cross, it is during the moments of what feels like the greatest abandonment that the most spiritual growth happens, unknown, imperceptible, but real. So the dark night of the soul is paradoxically not a time of despair. It is a time for the spirit to work on the soul, transforming the Beloved in the Lover – a night more lovely than the dawn.

I am not trying to encourage a masochistic embrace of pain. Suffering and pain are never, of themselves, good. It seems more than coincidental that the narrative of beneficial suffering applies so often to the powerless, not the powerful. Too often throughout history some people have been told to grin and bear it more than others. No. Dis-ease is the absence of ease, and suffering is the absence of joy.

But in the Christian story of Jesus Christ's arrest, condemnation, crucifixion and resurrection there can be no way to new life except through the encounter with death. We have to go into the darkness to find the light. The eye of the soul turns inwards, to the depths of the heart, and there it finds the infinity of the cosmos, held together by the light of love. There is a dazzling darkness at the heart of all life.

This is from Welsh poet Henry Vaughan:

> There is in God, some say,
>   A deep but dazzling darkness, as men here
>   Say it is late and dusky, because they
>   See not all clear.
>   O for that night! where I in Him
>   Might live invisible and dim![59]

The monk and mystic Thomas Merton prayed one Christmas Eve:

> Your brightness is my darkness. I know nothing of You and, by myself, I cannot even imagine how to go about knowing You. If I imagine You, I am mistaken. If I understand You, I am deluded. If I am conscious and certain I know You, I am crazy. The darkness is enough.[60]

It seems that there is life beyond black holes. It seems that some light can escape. The astronomer Carlo Crevelli's book *White Holes* suggests that as black holes decay they begin to release light again, and so the cosmos continues; the cycle of creation and destruction is not, after all, interrupted.

The final frontier in the spiritual journey is the reconciling of darkness and light. It can be a journey that lasts a lifetime. Its goal is the insight that, ultimately, everything is connected. Everything comes together. There is a deep unity underlying all things, expressed in the Islamic concept of *tawhid*, lying beneath Christian mystical spirituality, the infinite oneness of the Atman in Hindu cosmology. Darkness is as light to you.

***

In these chapters we have reflected on the body's fleshy materiality, and on nature's innumerable indifferences and awe-inspiring inventiveness. We have delved into the pain of lament and the delight of joy. We have considered the ultimate reality of death, and what lies on the other side of death, across the River Styx. And we have travelled towards that place where the light of the world and the land of deep darkness mutually create their dazzling enshadowed unity.

But where have we arrived? You may be feeling short-changed. You may be wondering whether it has all been worth it if all that we find at the foot of the rainbow are meaningless phrases. What can a 'dazzling darkness' or an 'invisible light' possibly mean? What's the point of pursuing a vision that has such an incomprehensible thing as its holy grail?

For a space rocket to escape from the earth's atmosphere it must have stages. Every rocket, when it's launched, bears its fuel with it in anything between two and five stages. Once the fuel is burnt, each stage is jettisoned. The rocket becomes lighter and can break free of the constraints of gravity and atmosphere. Perhaps not a perfect illustration in the context of the climate crisis – but the rocket needs the fuel to begin with, and then must leave it behind to break free.

Spiritual mentors and directors encourage a disciplined approach to prayer and meditation, along with reflection and reading and compassionate actions and working for justice in an unjust world. These make up the rocket fuel that powers the journey.

But there comes a point when even they must fall away, because they too can become obstacles, dead weights that keep us earthbound. We let go of everything we recognize and set out across the emptiness of the universe with nothing to hold us or keep us safe. This is the goal of the spiritual journey – it's what we're aiming for.

But the risk is that, when we reach it, we might look around and say, 'Well, I think I'm there. But is there a "there" there?' The answer, of course, is paradoxical. Yes and no. Now and not yet. Within and without. The dazzling darkness. The invisible light. The absent presence, the easy yoke, the untouchable reality, the unreachable centre. None of this makes logical sense and yet it describes the truth we seek.

So we turn now to look at what 'there' could possibly be, and how it frees us to live lives not of quiet desperation but of vibrant hope.

PART 3

Is there a 'there' there?

11

The maze of city streets

Dusk in February. Sunlight slants across the park, skeletal plane trees casting long shadows. A couple of crows, black against the shadows, peck coolly in the bins overflowing with food containers and disposable cups. The dog walkers have brought their cockapoos and bull terriers for the last walk of the day. A siren squeals by on the street between me and Waterloo Station as I sit silently on a bench, cold, wrapped up, watching the people go by, watching the people watching their dogs do their stuff, listening to the sound of the trains, seeing the evening light brighten in that moment before the sun leaves us for the night, enjoying the sounds, sights, smells, busy at the heart of the city, busy doing nothing, watching, listening, waiting, open. Twenty minutes of silence at the heart of the maelstrom.

How often people say that they have to go to the country to be spiritual. 'I find god in nature, I go to Scotland/the Himalayas/the Suffolk coast for my fix.' Which, I am sure, is true. But why must it be either/or? How has the belief taken root that to be spiritual we have to leave the smoke behind us and escape to the country, supposedly untouched by the smudge of trade or the smear of industry?

More widely, how has the belief taken root that spiritual knowledge is reserved only for particular kinds of people: contemplatives, monks, nuns, people who have renounced the world and taken the road less travelled, who have forsaken the predictable for the wilderness? It's not only in Christianity that renunciation and spiritual wisdom are believed to be inseparable. *Sannyasin* in Hindu cosmology are people who, having achieved material fulfilment, give everything away and make their way into the forest or on to the road, to rely on alms for life's necessities. In Islam,

Sufi saints are often people who lived hermit-like lives, far away from the crowds, seeking solace in silence.

Deep spirituality, true spirituality, mystical spirituality is apparently not for the likes of you and me. It's for special people, set apart by God. The best-known English mystic, Mother Julian of Norwich, was an anchorite – she had herself walled up in her cell until she died there. St Teresa of Avila was a nun. Rumi renounced the world in order to be with his beloved.

But this narrative is not as clear-cut as it seems. Yes, spending day after day in worship, prayer and work, living simply on the road relying on handouts to survive, all this may help create a deep spiritual awareness. But it isn't necessarily the only way, and if we look more closely at the lives of Mother Julian or St Teresa or Rumi we find a very different story.

Julian's shrine in Norwich includes a replica of her cell (the original church of St Julian was destroyed in World War Two). In the south wall is a large window which looks out on to what is now a quiet street. But when the woman (we do not know her name: she is called Julian after the shrine where she lived) was living there, it was a main route to the local market. She spent much time talking with passers-by and people who came from far and wide to speak with her. Her writings are gloriously physical and she has a great eye for colour. She writes:

> For as the body is clad in the cloth, and the flesh in the skin, and the bones in the flesh, and the heart in the trunk, so are we, soul and body, clad and enclosed in the goodness of God.[61]

Describing her Second Revelation, she writes that her vision was

> Suddenly let down into the bottom of the sea, and there I saw green hills and valleys, with the appearance of moss strewn with seaweed and gravel.[62]

She writes of the blood of Christ as shifting in tone from 'brownish red' to 'bright red' and of the roundness of the drops as being like herrings' scales. St Teresa was a super-abbess of many convents and lived a complex life, fending off resistance as she and her friend and colleague St John of the Cross tried to reform their part of the Carmelite order. Rumi was already a jurist, a preacher and a teacher. After his encounter with Shams he continued to teach and preach, and wrote his great poem, *The Masnavi*, to channel a new level of spiritual insight.

The notion that mystical or spiritual experience is only for special people is wrong-headed. Many who have inspired thousands worked out their spiritual paths in the middle of great busyness. Meister Eckhart, of whom more later, was one of only two people to hold the Chair of Theology in Paris twice (the other was Thomas Aquinas). He was administrator of a province of the Dominican order and preached and taught in the vernacular, especially to women who lived in the Béguine communities in the northern Rhine area. In the middle of a hectic life he opened up a radically new vision of God, drawing on the traditions of centuries but expressing it in ways that remain fresh and innovative today.

Mother Julian or Rumi or Meister Eckhart did not consider themselves to be 'mystics' or call their experiences 'mystical'. The wisdom they discovered through prayer and work, reading, self-denial and worship was the distillation of their experience of a god who revealed godself in ways that were at once incomprehensible and utterly real. Margery Kempe had the gift of tears and would wail loudly in her prayers. Teresa had the gift of levitation, often after the Eucharist and to her great irritation. But both were determinedly ordinary. The paths into deep spiritual awareness are open to all whether they live in the middle of a town or in a cell in the depths of the forest.

The Bible, famously, starts in a garden and ends in a city. The final book, Revelation, ends with a description of the City of God:

> I saw the holy city, the new Jerusalem, coming down out of heaven from God, prepared as a bride adorned for her husband. And I heard a loud voice from the throne saying,
> 'See, the home of God is among mortals.
> He will dwell with them;
> they will be his peoples,

and God himself will be with them;
he will wipe every tear from their eyes.
Death will be no more;
mourning and crying and pain will be no more,
for the first things have passed away.' (Rev. 21.2–4)

Wiliam Blake saw angels in a tree on Peckham Rye in south London. He lived in Hercules Road, not far from St John's, Waterloo, and wrote some of his best-known poems there. The dark Satanic mills of the poem 'Jerusalem' are the factories belching smoke along the riverbank painted by Monet 80 years later in his paintings of the Thames.

A meaningful journey into a nourishing spirituality involves both busyness and quiet, both community and privacy, both noise and silence. It's certainly important to spend time away from the crowds. But it's also important to be engaged, to experience the challenges and joys of everyday life and to find the light of the spirit in the eyes of the people we meet.

Madeleine Delbrêl was born in the south of France in 1904. She grew up an atheist but in 1924 in Paris, when her fiancé became a Dominican, she had a conversion experience. She read the writings of St Teresa and began to keep silence for five minutes a day. She found her way to a small town on the outskirts of Paris called Ivry-sur-Seine. She kept a house open to everyone, finding God in the daily encounters with the poor and vulnerable of the town, writing, reading, praying and entering into the challenges facing those around her. She lived in Ivry for the rest of her life, dying of a brain haemorrhage in 1964.

She was convinced that the Spirit was to be found in the lives of the people of the street. In her book *The Holiness of Ordinary People*, she writes:

> From a sand dune, dressed in white, the [traditional] missionary overlooks an expanse of lands filled with unbaptised peoples. From the top of a long subway staircase, dressed in an ordinary suit or raincoat, we [ordinary people] overlook, on each step, during this busy rush-hour time, an expanse of heads, of bustling heads, waiting for the door to open. Caps,

berets, hats, and hair of every colour. Hundreds of heads – hundreds of souls. And there we stand, above. And above us, and everywhere, is God.[63]

In *We The Ordinary People of the Streets*, she says:

We, the ordinary people of the streets, believe with all our might that this street, this world, where God has placed us, is our place of holiness.[64]

Our place of holiness. I am writing this in a vicarage in Waterloo, in the middle of a hectic day of meetings and administration, reading, praying and leading a Eucharist service. I've been in this parish for 15 years. As I often say, if you were to cut London out and balance it on a pin, the pin would be down the road from the church, near the Old Vic Theatre – so St John's is right at the heart of London. It's a busy place where people are constantly coming and going, where challenges arise every day. But it's also a place of prayer, and silence, and reflection, a place where the Spirit is able to breathe and move, a place to which people come in order to deepen their relationship with the divine, to reach out towards the infinite. To explore spirituality.

So I resonate with Meister Eckhart, who must occasionally have given sermons without much preparation, who must have been pushed for time to pray, who must have sometimes felt that the world was too much with him. I resonate with Rumi, teaching all week and finding time in the evening to write his poems by the light of a guttering candle. I resonate with Mother Julian, dispensing unexpected advice to a passer-by in distress when she had set an hour or two aside intending to spend time in silent prayer. And I resonate with the members of the congregation here, many of whom live complicated lives but manage to find a way of nourishing their spiritual awareness and creating a deep relationship with the mystical reality that we know as God.

As Cole Arthur Riley says,

The chasm between the spiritual and the physical is no greater than that between a thought and a word. They cannot be disconnected. And it is difficult to tell where one ends and the other begins, perhaps because there is no such place.⁶⁵

Our spiritual lives are both defined by and define the material worlds in which we live. Different cultures and different times in history have produced amazingly diverse expressions of spiritual experience, from the quietly Anglican spirituality of St John's, Waterloo, to the wild joy in, say, huge Sufi gatherings in Sudan or Tanzania. One of the most powerful accounts of an encounter with the spiritual that I have read is by Malidoma Patrice Somé, who grew up in a Dagara village in West Africa and was abducted as a child by Catholic missionaries. He was kept in a Catholic mission until his early teens when he escaped and made his way back to the village, where he was (reluctantly, as some of the elders mistrusted him) allowed to take part in the coming-of-age rituals of the village. *Of Water and the Spirit* describes his experience of slipping from the visible to the invisible, meeting the spirits of his ancestors.⁶⁶ Somé became an interpreter of Dagara culture to the West, having a foot in both the post-Enlightenment Catholic and the indigenous African worlds.

Moments of transcendent stillness, looking out over infinite distances framed by the silhouettes of mountains enshadowed by the light of the setting sun – these are rare in the urban jungle. But wherever we are, city or mountain, there are flickers of inspiration when we see the light of love in the gaze of a person we are speaking to, or capture a second of silence in the discipline of daily prayer. There is often a moment of what sociologist Emile Durkheim calls 'collective effervescence' at St John's on a Sunday morning, in the quiet after everyone has received Communion.

The tradition of urban mystics such as Madeleine Delbrêl lives on in the creativity of hip-hop, tracing its roots directly back to Pentecostal worship among Black communities in the streets of Southside Chicago and south London. Alejandro Nava, Professor of Religious Studies at the University of Arizona, delves into the spiritual ancestry of hip-hop in *Street Scriptures: Between God and Hip-Hop*:

Hip-hop is a reclamation of the ancient tradition of poetics, a return to the time when the spoken word was the vital breath and soul of a culture, its power mysterious and magical. It resurrects the musicality that once swaddled the Word in Jewish, Christian and Greco-Roman poetics, an eloquence that aimed for the heart as much as for the mind.[67]

If you are in any doubt about that, listen to Kendrick Lamar's album *Damn*, with its powerful lyrics reflecting on the intersection between Black male America and the God of the Bible – for example, 'HUMBLE', 'FEAR' and 'GOD'.

Spiritual exploration is deeply communal. It's possible to be 'spiritual but not religious' but the solo journey is far harder. That's why spirituality and religion are inextricably intertwined. Religious practice is the clothing on the spiritual body.

Pilgrims walk alongside one another on the Camino to Santiago di Compostella. The encounters they have are some of the most inspiring parts of their quest. Ancient religious traditions survive because they tell of the journey towards the infinite in, yes, a bewildering diversity of ways and with accretions of exclusivity and judgement which are painful to see, but the wisdom of centuries is contained in the stories and actions of Sufi or Jewish or Hindu or Christian worship. The challenge is to find the transformative nuggets in the layers of tradition.

Henry, Francesca and Deepti dared to cross our threshold and take part in our worship. They came because they were looking for a place where they could ask the questions they wanted to ask. Who or what is god, and how can I live a life that is grounded and meaningful? They wanted to be with others who are asking the same questions. Worshipping communities at their best are seedbeds of spiritual wisdom where you can put down roots and grow towards the incandescent light of love.

12

Mountains of the mind

Imagine that you've tried your hardest to follow the path. You've creatively celebrated the spiritual in nature, you've encouraged your body and your spirit to speak in harmony, you've heard the lament of the powerless and the unjustly treated, you've meditated on your death, you've embraced the darkness. You feel that you are close to understanding this yearning towards the infinite.

Then you come across these words of Meister Eckhart:

> We pray to God that we may be free of God.[68]

Or you read the fourteenth-century text *The Cloud of Unknowing* and are dismayed to find:

> Whoever hears or reads about all this, and thinks that it is fundamentally an activity of the mind, and proceeds then to work it all out along these lines, is on quite the wrong track. He manufactures an experience that is neither spiritual nor physical. He is dangerously missed and in real peril.[69]

And:

> See to it that there is nothing at work in your mind or will but only God. Try to suppress all knowledge and feeling of anything less than God, and trample it down deep under the cloud of forgetting.[70]

Perhaps it makes you feel like giving up and going shopping. But stay with it, because we are reaching the most exciting part of the spiritual journey. A fine biography of Eckhart by Joel Harrington is called *Dangerous Mystic: Meister Eckhart's Path to the God*

Within. The Meister, says Harrington, was dangerous because he taught:

- Mystical experience was not reserved for religious professionals, for monks, nuns and priests. It was, and is, available for everyone who is willing to take the step of unsaying, unlearning, all that they think they know of god; to become free of god that they may see god.
- The spiritual path is unsettling, unfixed. The ground is not solid and the Rock of Ages is queasily unstable. He often speaks of gelâzenheit, 'letting-go-ness' – freeing, becoming free, releasing God from the box in which we have locked god.
- Everyone contains a spark of the divine, waiting to burst into a self-consuming holy fire.

Eckhart was not the first to believe that we could say nothing about god that is true. St Augustine said, 'If you understand, it is not God.'[71] *Mystical Theology*, by another anonymous author known as Pseudo-Dionysius, who was born in the late fifth century, prays:

> Guide us to that topmost height of mystic lore which exceeds light and more than exceeds knowledge, where the simple, absolute, and unchangeable mysteries of heavenly Truth lie hidden in the dazzling obscurity of the secret Silence, outshining all brilliance with the intensity of their darkness, and surcharging our blinded intellects with the utterly impalpable and invisible fairness of glories which exceed all beauty![72]

At the beginning of Chapter II, he prays:

> Unto this Darkness which is beyond Light we pray that we may come, and may attain unto vision through the loss of sight and knowledge, and that in ceasing thus to see or to know we may learn to know that which is beyond all perception and understanding.

Ali, the nephew of the prophet Muhammad, is regarded by Sufis as the spiritual foundation of the mystical path of wisdom passed down by the Prophet. He is reported to have said this:

Know that all the wisdom of the Heavenly Scriptures are in the Qur'an and whatever is in the Qur'an is in the Fatiha (Suratul Hamd) and whatever is in the Fatiha is in Bismillah and whatever is in Bismillah is in the 'Ba' of Bismillah and whatever is in the 'Ba' of Bismillah is encapsulated in the dot under 'Ba'; and I am that dot under 'Ba'.[73]

The Fatiha is the opening verse of the Qur'an: 'Bismilla ar-Rahman ar-Raheem' – 'In the name of God, the infinitely compassionate and merciful.' Bismi – in the name of – in Arabic is بسم. The first letter, reading from right to left, has a dot under it. Ali the prophet tells us that he is the dot, for he contains within himself all the mystery and all the truth of the Qur'an.

The poet, scholar and mystic Ibn Arabi was born in Andalusia in 1165. He travelled widely throughout the Muslim world and died in Damascus in 1240. Some say that he is second only to the Prophet Muhammad in the pantheon of Muslim figures. His best-known work is a reflection on the lives of many of the prophets – *Fusus Al-hikam*: *The Bezels* [or *Ringstones*] *of Wisdom*.

The opening chapter of the book reflects on Adam, the first prophet, who is, according to Ibn Arabi, the perfect human, revealing the mystery of God as if through the polishing of a mirror. Adam is the polishing, as a result of which he disappears, so only the reflection of the divine is manifest. The perfect human, Adam, is the invisible isthmus between the mystery of Allah and the daily concrete reality of the world.

A white-blazed gazelle is an amazing sight,
Red-dye signaling, eyelids hinting,
Pasture between breathlessness and innards.
Wonder, a garden among the flames!

My heart can take on any form:
A meadow for gazelles,
A cloister for monks.

For the idols, sacred ground,
Ka'ba for the circling pilgrim

The tables of the Torah,
The scrolls of the Qur'an.

I profess the religion of love
Wherever its caravan turns along the way.[74]

Ibn Arabi is part of a mystical tradition that includes Meister Eckhart and his close contemporary Marguerite de Porete. There are powerful correspondences between their writings, for all three follow the Neoplatonist schools of thought and understand the divine to be so far beyond our imagination that we cannot even speak of it. God is both infinitely close and infinitely distant, and we humans are drawn into god by the spirit until there is no distinction between human and divine. All is one. The transcendent collapses into the immanent and the immanent expands into the transcendent. The ultimately real, which gives life and meaning to the visible world, is comprehensible only when time and space lose all significance and we become mystically united with the divine who is beyond words. As the Qur'an says, 'We [Allah] are closer to them than their jugular vein.'[75]

If all this makes little sense, please don't worry. Eckhart preached many sermons in vernacular German rather than church Latin so that lay people could understand. He worked closely with women who were members of Béguine communities in Northern Europe. He knew that he was pushing at the boundaries of spiritual experience, and he often tried to encourage his hearers by reassuring them that if his sermons weren't clear, they should not be anxious; the path will lead them on, if they allow it, and things will become clearer in due course.

To find the truth of love, we have to let go of the truth of love. There is a space within and beyond the cosmos which is neither time nor space, where light and dark have no meaning: non-being, the Atman, the deep soul, the Yogic state of trigunatita, the state beyond the limitations of being, the divine tawhid (unity). In that space our deepest selves are united with the deepest being of the cosmos.

I find myself disappearing into mystical speech. Good. Here's the paradox: the immanent and the transcendent are one. The

God who is present is the God who is absent, and to have a rich spirituality is to merge the vertical and the horizontal, the apophatic and the kataphatic, the now and the not yet. We need both apophatic and kataphatic, both absence and presence, both spirit within and spirit beyond. To unlock the wisdom of children we need to embrace our adulthood and understand how we have become the people we are, so that we can discover the authentic self within us which is god.

This is the heart of the matter, where boundaries between material and spiritual are blurred and pliable, and where Enlightenment rationalism is transformed by spiritual wisdom.

Spiritual practice is like piano practice; day after day of struggle is necessary so that the end result seems effortless. Great pianists are unconscious of their technique as they play; they are conscious only of the music they are making. Great spiritual teachers are, at moments of intense awareness, unconscious of the chains and ropes that bind them to the world. They are conscious only of the fleeting infinity which is god. Neither great musicianship nor deep spiritual wisdom are learnt without decades of practice.

And trust. A pianist takes her seat at the piano in the Albert Hall, with the orchestra behind her and the conductor beside her. When the orchestra has finished the introduction and the moment comes when she must begin to play, she has to trust her fingers, her body and her soul to come together to create that moment of music which inspires the 6,000 people sitting in the hall.

There are things whereof we cannot speak, said the philosopher Ludwig Wittgenstein, and of those we must keep silent. The fire of silence and stillness is the fire at which we can warm our hearts – if we are willing to let go of our desire for warmth and the instinct that tells us to open our hearts. The heart will be opened by the working of the spirit, if we put ourselves in the arena, so that the work can happen in ways that are beyond our control and beyond our understanding. We can, by degrees, learn to unsay all the spiritual language we have learnt to use. It's a huge challenge, the process of unsaying, but it is an essential step – or non-step or un-step or de-step.

I struggle through the forest and I come out in a clearing. In front of me is the edge of a cliff. I can't go back into the forest.

I don't want to return to the arid wilderness away from which I have trekked for decades. I want to take flight. I want to lose myself in the eternal now, and in losing myself I want to find myself; for we do not find ourselves by seeking ourselves. We find ourselves by seeking god.

I have to take a leap of faith, out, out, out, over the abyss. I must trust that the angels will bear me up and bring me into the dazzling darkness of the eternal now. I must trust in spiritual weightlessness, the outworking of years of burrowing into the bloody guts and dark intestines, the scarlet blood and the radical temptations which have been the staging posts on my journey into the infinite at the epicentre of my being.

I think of a woman I met on a Palestinian solidarity march in early 2025. Marcia had come up from Croydon and told me as she danced to the drums of the shouted slogans that she attended a Pentecostal church. I watched her dancing in anger and hope, calling for an end to the bombings, hoping against hope for a lasting and reconstructive ceasefire. If I had spoken to her about the unmoved mover, the paradox at the heart of divinity, God as the uncreated one, us as humans needing to decreate, to 'nothing' ourselves (Mother Julian's verb) as God is 'nothinged', I think she would have understood, because I think that is what she experiences, week after week, as her bodily and spiritual worship merge in the physicality of dance, of call and response, of 'Yes, brother!' and 'Say it, sister!' She sings the song of liberation, the song that Baby Suggs sang in the clearing with the children and the women and the men in the Deep South before slavery was abolished.

Urban mysticism. It's not a grand or a dramatic thing, but as I write this, hearing the trains rumbling across the Waterloo viaduct, it makes sense. Many mystics downplay the importance of dramatic visions. A young novice rushed up to Teresa of Avila in a state of great excitement because she had had a vision of angels and the heavenly host and God revealing themselves to her – she had been transported, and wanted to tell the Mother Superior of the amazing experience she had been given. 'Very good, my dear,' said the saint. 'Keep praying. It will soon pass.'

Mother Julian had one night of 'seeings' when she was very ill and it seemed that she might die. She spent the rest of her life in prayer and reflection, but the visions did not come again.

This quiet sense of the absent presence, the impossibly distant absolute which is encompassed by the human heart, this deep reality which enfolds you and me and all we can see in the undifferentiated infinity which lies at the core of everything we can see or sense – this is the end of the quest for the spiritual. Yet it is also the beginning, for it is a place (not really a place) where time and space have no meaning, and so everything – past, present and future – is contained in the room that is not a room, beyond the doors that are not doors, where the darkness is dazzling, where infinite love is the spark that lights the fire that burns for ever and consumes nothing.

Mystical experience is routine, real, everyday. It's a manifestation of the quotidian, radical relationship between us and the godhead. None of this is special, and yet all of it is beyond special. We have to let go to find; the letting go is an act of commitment.

I invite you to carry out a thought experiment. Imagine that the trees are the dwelling places of the spirit, that the walls of your house and the streetlights in your road and the dogs and cats and foxes which have their homes in the streets around you are also manifestations of the divine. That god is present and active, dynamic and alive, in the moving of the planets and the beating of your heart. That everything, everywhere, all at once, is made of light and the infinite vibration of infinitesimal pulses of something which is both wave and particle, which is and is not matter, which is and is not spirit.

Imagine that you are seeing a world that is enchanted, which is transformative, which is in relationship with you and you with it; not an objectified thing fit only to be exploited, but a world that receives and returns your love and your hopes and your dreams. Imagine that you are caught up in a cosmic dance and all that you do, all that you think, all that you are, is bound up with the world around you in ways you can barely begin to understand.

How does that feel? Scary and silly? Or different? Good? Exciting?

13

God is a verb

I've accepted that the whole of my life will be a pilgrimage toward the sound of the genuine in me. This may sound troubling to those who've been conditioned to believe that our journey is to God and God alone, but I say the two paths are one. My journey to the truth of God cannot be parsed from my journey to the truth of who I am. A fidelity to the true self is a fidelity to truth. I won't apologize for this. (Cole Arthur Riley, *This Here Flesh*)[76]

St John's, Waterloo, was built in 1824 in the neoclassical style based on the Parthenon. The front of the church is a massive portico, held up by six pillars. They hold up the roof and create a space where people can come and go, laugh and cry, pray and sing and be themselves.

The spiritual journey never ends. It is a spiral, endlessly turning away from the Infinite and finding its way back in. It is the slow revolution of galaxies through the cosmos. Nothing is still. The journey is motion, flow, flux. It is made up of call and response, always on the point of unbalancing but always held in tension. Within many Eastern traditions the cycle is one of birth, death and reincarnation. Within Christianity the cycle is encapsulated in the image of the Trinity – three modes of God in relationship with one another, as in the famous icon by Andrei Rublev – and in God's relationship with humanity, God's hand reaching across the void towards the finger of Adam.

Relationships need work. They are unstable and have to be carefully nourished or they die. God is not god unless god is in relationship with the world, for god is love and love cannot exist without an object to love. Love is offer and receipt, and the strange thing about love is that the more it is given, the more there is to give.

Nothing is as solid as it seems. A brick, a star, a human heart are all made up of infinitesimal bursts of energy interacting with each other in ways we do not yet understand. Neutrons and protons and quarks and neutrinos and all the other subatomic particles or waves, which are not really waves or particles at all but tiny bursts of quantum energy, are perpetually in reaction with each other, and by a miracle the zillions of interactions that take place every millisecond combine to produce the stability of molecules and atoms, which in equally miraculous ways combine to form bricks and stars and hearts.

Energy is constantly giving itself to the energy around it, and through these fragile cosmic donations things we can touch and feel come into being and combine and combine and combine to form moving, living beings who can conceive the cosmos, name it, dream it, pray about it, at times destroy it and at others love it.

The pillars of St John's are massive. They have stood for 200 years, and I hope they will stand for another 200 years. They are made up of those infinitely small cosmic processes; the structure is strong but consists of tiny episodes of vulnerability. The static world is a world of action. Nothing is really static, everything is in movement, even the Spirit.

God is a verb.

Outside my window, seagulls are circling high above Waterloo Station, riding the air currents; if they stop, they stall and crash to the ground. It may help make sense of Meister Eckhart's mysterious call to free ourselves of god so that we may see god if we understand that everything is in motion. Nothing that appears real is really as real as it appears. Perhaps the god we are asking to be free from is the god who is static, unchanging, unflinching, harsh, solid, the God of judgement and of the past, the God who holds in his (nearly always his) hand the lightbeams of heaven and the thunderbolts of doom and hell.

Too often, religions are seen as presenting god as a straitjacket and faith as a prison. Constancy and stability and materiality are good things, of course. They enable us to build buildings and eat and wear clothes and create and embrace, and they enable us pass on wisdom and guidance and customs from one generation to the next so that communities can survive and even thrive. St John's needs its pillars so that the roof is a roof and not a floor. But stability is not good if it becomes a straitjacket, and materiality is not good if it creates the bars of a prison.

Letting go of the god we think we understand removes the ground from under the feet of those who would use religion to justify exclusion or violence towards others. A distorted notion of god has been coopted many times by the powers and principalities of this world to support ideological positions that are oppressive or unjust, to support nationalist or racist or homophobic actions – Hindu nationalism, the Christian Right in the USA, LGBTQI+ exclusion, religious justifications for settler colonialism, apartheid, genocide.

This is why it is so vital (literally, life-giving) that the spiritual journey is one that allows streams of living water to flow into the river from many sources. Ibn Arabi drew inspiration from Andalusian and Eastern Sufi mystics, from Islamic schools of jurisprudence, from Jewish Kabbalistic thought and from Christian Gnostic teachings. He was also familiar with Buddhist and Hindu teachings: a Persian translation of a Sanskrit work on tantric yoga has been attributed to him. 'In this connection, his important theory of the Creative Imagination bears a striking resemblance to the Hindu concept of maya.'[77]

God is a verb, and so are you, and so am I.

Great spiritual leaders are marked by their humility. They point beyond themselves to a greater reality – towards the infinite – and they do not seek recognition for its own sake. Too many of us, me included, seek safety through accumulating power. We pretend to give, or we give when it is safe to give, unwilling to take risks, unwilling to reflect the love we have received and to live truly generous lives. We do not trust the notion that in giving, we receive. Self-emptying – kenosis – is a scary idea, and it feels hard to build the confidence to do it. Archbishop Desmond Tutu or Nelson Mandela or Madeleine Debrêl were not seeking adulation or glory. On the contrary, they gave of themselves unstintingly for the sake of those around them, wherever they found themselves.

How are we to be strong and grow in the journey we are making, as Tutu and Mandela and Debrêl grew into their own fullness? I offer six pillars of practice, corresponding with the six pillars of St John's, to help you unlock the intangible depths and the dazzling darkness of spiritual wisdom. Paradox alert: once again, we're slipping into a world where the ground is uncertain; we are building a house on unsolid rock, but the house will stand if it is built on deep foundations.

First: be silent. Even in the midst of urban busyness – especially in the midst of urban busyness – be silent. Find a moment, a few moments, a few minutes, 20 minutes, every day if you can, to sit silently. Perhaps when you wake up, if there are no children needing breakfast or there is no commute demanding your time. Or, if there are children needing breakfast, perhaps on your way to work once they've been despatched to their places of learning. Or, if you can find a quiet place during the day, a park, a church (if it's open), a space – not necessarily totally silent but at the very least away from too much hubbub – sit, for a time, maybe set your alarm, and be silent.

Why? Because mystical experience, whether urban or rural, is grounded in silence. The Eastern mystics, students of Kabbala, monks, Sufis, Jesus, the Buddha, Muhammad, so many, all spent days or weeks or months or even years in silence. It's not necessary to head for the highlands to find the spirit, but it is necessary to go into a quiet place and set your alarm for a manageable period, and then shut up.

You might find it helpful to repeat a mantra, a short phrase. Many Christians use the word 'maranatha', the Aramaic word for 'come, Lord, come'. Others repeat the Jesus prayer: 'Lord Jesus Christ, Son of the Living God, have mercy on me.' Or you could follow the Dharmic tradition and repeat a cosmic sound such as om.

You will find that most of the time your thoughts are like an anthill. Mine certainly are. If I set the alarm for 25 minutes, I know that I will be repeating my mantra (maranatha) for about five minutes. The rest of the time I am planning my day or responding to emails in my head or making up devastating one-liners to be used against someone who annoyed me three weeks ago. No matter. Keep on turning up, keep on making the time. For me, silence is simply a way of getting out of the way, clearing the woods, opening up the cupboard so that the divine, the Spirit, can do her work. The tectonic plates begin to shift, often imperceptibly, but they shift nonetheless; silence is golden because it makes a space for the light to shine into the world.

Second: pray. Pray, even if you aren't sure what you're praying to, even if you find the idea of god difficult, even if you think you don't know how to pray and other people seem to understand it so much better, just pray. Prayer is, very simply, the opening up of the channel between you and the divine power which underlies everything, life, light, god, call it what you will. There are formal ways of praying – five times a day, facing towards Mecca, with carefully prescribed gestures – or there are informal ways of praying – lying in bed, chatting to god, spitting out a few words while you are on your bike on the way to college or office. Prayer, like god, is a verb. Prayer enables spiritual movement. It creates a dynamic between the now and the not yet, the here and the infinitely not here, the material and the spiritual. Prayer is a conversation, and like all conversations it can take a bewildering range of forms. Fine. Let it be varied, let it be perplexing, but above all let it be regular. If you can, find a community to pray with, either online or near your home or work. Keep on turning up.

Third: read. By which I mean absorb, voraciously, all the wisdom of our forebears and those who are writing now, or speaking, or making Instagram posts, or creating music that speaks to you. Listen to Kendrick Lamar and Schubert, read Mother Julian and Thich Nath Hanh, listen to a podcast (Generous Faith is good, produced by St John's, Waterloo); read accounts of the life of the Prophet Muhammad, listen to David Suchet reading the Bible. Enjoy the poetry of Mary Oliver, who allows the natural world to speak of the spirit. There are an infinite number of ways to receive the wisdom of the centuries and of the world, so there will always be more to discover. If you don't know where to start, ask for advice or look at the reading list at the end of this book. Just read.

And, while you're reading – or praying, or being silent, or listening – put your phone to one side. Please. Switch off your notifications and set your device to silent. The spiritual journey needs focus and commitment. It stands against the short-term distractions of TikTok or Instagram or Facebook, or whatever in the vortex of virtual time supplants them. My experience of social media is that it rarely builds us up and nourishes our spirits. More often it distracts, diminishes, produces feelings of envy or FOMO. Doomscrolling – the clue's in the name. The internet is a magical tool for finding information and contacts, but for unlocking wisdom? Very much less so. Treat it with caution.

Fourth: give. Give generously. Give of everything you have received: time, love, money, possessions, thoughtfulness, hope, fear, food. Maybe not like Vincent Van Gogh, who as a young man tried to be a priest until his family brought him home as he insisted on giving everything away all the time. As Jesus says in the Sermon on the Mount, if you have two coats, give one. Share your food with those who are hungry. Give of your time, making sure you keep enough to be nourished yourself, to receive more so that you can give more.

Remember that spirituality is subversive. Give of your passion. If you are passionate about justice or climate or housing and homelessness or birds or any of the myriad ways in which people and nature are under threat or being oppressed, be inspired by your sense of injustice or loss to take action, to be a political animal, to play your part in the public square.

Society, community, family – they all need us. Giving is a doing word and the idea of gift is intrinsic to spiritual maturity. Through giving we receive, and if we give what we receive we have more room to give more.

> 'Do not judge, and you will not be judged; do not condemn, and you will not be condemned. Forgive, and you will be forgiven; give, and it will be given to you. A good measure, pressed down, shaken together, running over, will be put into your lap;

for the measure you give will be the measure you get back.'
(Luke 6.37–38)

Think about light. Darkness is the absence of light and what we see is the result of objects returning light to us – giving it away. The brighter a light, the more energy it is giving away.

We are what we give. When we receive love, we can cling on to it or we can give it away. When we receive joy, hope, generosity, spirit, we can cling on to it or we can give it away. Life is a mirror, and what we reflect affects our relationships with the world around us. A dark mirror has no function and no purpose. If we sit lightly to what we receive, we can redirect the gifts we are given in a constant round of generosity of spirit and play a deeper part in the cosmic conversation.

Fifth: listen. Without listening, nothing will change. Listen to the voices beyond the voices you can hear. Listen for the music beyond the music you hear. The music of the spheres, the voice of the darkness, the words of the voiceless, the still small voice, the murmuring sound beneath the grinding of the earthquake. Listen in the silence to what your heart is telling you. Listen to the voices beneath your heart, which may be saying things that feel uncomfortable, things you really would rather not hear. Listen to the spirit as she moves.

This is, for many, one of the most challenging pillars. It certainly is for me. I can set time aside for silence relatively easily. I can find time for prayer. I would happily read and learn for 25 hours a day. I have space for giving and volunteering. But the avalanche of things that need doing, people who need attention, messages that need responses, social media that needs me to read it and react, lists that need making – all of this gets in the way of quietly listening and carefully hearing what the divine, the spirit, is saying.

There is little that is harder than the deep dive into the real – not least because our self-protective souls would often like to avoid hearing the home truths which the spirit might be pointing out to us: the selfish motives we have for wanting to appear kind, thoughtful or generous; the insidious competitiveness which is in all of us and comes out so clearly in timelines on Facebook, masquerading as humble pride or surprised delight in our achievements. If we listen to the deepest voices, beyond the depths of our hearts, we may understand our prevarications and our petulances better; but these are shameful things, hard to admit, and so we often prefer to drown ourselves in busyness rather than face the truths that are forged in the crucible of self-awareness.

Sometimes it can be good to have a friend to help you listen. There is a useful discipline in Christianity known as spiritual direction, where a trained guide accompanies you on the journey, helping you to ask difficult questions or pointing you in directions that may be fruitful. Within Sufi traditions many people gather around particular sheikhs. In India, a guru is a spiritual guide who can both challenge and inspire.

My own experience of receiving and offering spiritual direction has been humbling. I have been challenged: 'Giles, if you're really going to make progress in this you have to be willing to set aside more than ten minutes a day.' And I have challenged others: 'Where is the spirit in all of this? What are you really hearing?' Sometimes a question as simple as that, and then a silent waiting for answers, can produce startling honesty and spiritual insights.

Sixth: share. Share the journey. All of this is much more productive if you can find kindred spirits with whom to share your delights and your struggles. It's not an accident that religion is a communal activity, and worship is almost always carried out by a congregation (literally, a 'stepping together'). Churches, mosques, synagogues, temples are places where people gather for a reason. On a very basic level, serotonin is released through acting or singing in unison. But beyond that, sharing the journey in friendship, often with people who are outside our comfort zones or from a wider demographic than our friends and families, can bring moments of support and moments of challenge that inspire and transform. If there are no physical communities you find amenable near your home, then try finding a community online – there are reliable and trustworthy groups of spiritual seekers working together online as much as in person. Sharing the liturgy (the 'work of the people') is a creative way to learn, to change and to grow.

This is not to undermine the practice of withdrawing from the world, of becoming a hermit, a way of life that has been honoured through the centuries. Some are called to be hermits, just as some are called to be celibate. But many are not. A solitary way of life is hugely difficult and not for the faint-hearted.

Of course there are risks with religious communities. They can quickly become rigid, unchanging, conservative, or be dominated by small groups of powerful people. The frequency of abuse, emotional and sexual, is heartbreaking. All communities can become sclerotic and corrosive. But at their best, and if the spirit is allowed to move and to speak and to bring about change, religious communities and congregations are places that offer times of holding and times of inspiration, of deep nourishment in joy and in sorrow.

Religious traditions all have their own ways of marking the calendar through shared fasting and celebration – Yom Kippur, Holi, Ramadan. Feasts and festivals resonate with our own rhythms of life. The liturgical round of the Christian year, from Advent through the joy of Christmas into the simplicity of Lent and the dark story of Holy Week, culminating in the brightness of the resurrection at Easter ... it's a story that bears repeating year after year after year. Try it. It works.

***

If you build these pillars carefully and with commitment, changes will happen. They offer tools for a different life, maps for the journey through the forest. It might be helpful for you to write down your intentions and combine them into a Rule of Life or Rhythm of Life – something that has been part of the spiritual journey for centuries, often modelled on the great Rule of St Benedict which transformed monastic life in the fifth century and has been used and imitated thousands of times since. A Rule of Life can be a simple thing, setting out achievable intentions – ten minutes of silence in the morning, giving away a certain percentage of your income (often 10 per cent), taking exercise, going to worship, and so on. It's useful, as something to refer to, perhaps annually, and revise as you travel further into the forest.

At the heart of all this remains the paradox to which I have often returned in this book, the paradox that is impossible to put into words and yet must be spoken, for it is the keystone of this structure we are building.

All of this, all this work, these silences, this praying, giving, reading, listening, sharing, this Rule of Life, this travelling along the spiritual path – it's all necessary and good. Celebrating creation and nature, expressing lament and joy, reflecting on life and death, light and darkness – it's all necessary and good.

But there comes a point where we have to leave the forest and move on to the trackless plane, where nothing is real and nothing is certain because there seems to be nothing there, and even nothing is no-thing and cannot be spoken. The mystery at the very core of the spiritual journey is that we are moving towards a state of emptiness, of non-being, of existence beyond existence which can never be comprehended.

We struggle through thickets that clutch at our feet, or spend time walking across carpets of pine needles beneath gnarled Scotch pines, or make our way through the foothills and scramble up across rocks and scree, ridge over ridge, to reach the goal; and when we reach the goal we do indeed find that what we were looking for is not there at all. There is no 'there' there; and yet, what is there is more real than anything we can touch or see. That's why we call it god.

14

Here I am!

It's not a surprise that most religious traditions teach that deep spirituality can only be unlocked through serious application and thought. The Higher Way and the Lower Way in Buddhism with their complicated paths, the Spiritual Exercises of St Ignatius Loyola, the mysteries of the Kabbala – all these have come into being because leaders and teachers have understood that the path is slippery and tortuous, mysterious and challenging.

It's easier to follow the will-o'-the-wisp across the marsh and sink into the bog than to pick our way through the quagmire towards the more solid ground on the other side. We are created human, with the human capacity to embrace beauty and hope, to feel fear and lament. To be fully human is to reach towards infinity. St Irenaeus famously said, 'The glory of God is a human being fully alive'; but the second half of that sentence, rarely quoted, reads 'and to be alive consists in beholding God'.[78]

What's essential is a moment of decision. An acknowledgement that we are only tiny parts of a wider, deeper, ineffable whole. A decision to join the dancers in a cosmic dance greater and more complex than anything we can imagine.

> There the angel of the Lord appeared to him in a flame of fire out of a bush; he looked, and the bush was blazing, yet it was not consumed. Then Moses said, 'I must turn aside and look at this great sight, and see why the bush is not burned up.' When the Lord saw that he had turned aside to see, God called to him out of the bush, 'Moses, Moses!' And he said, 'Here I am.' (Ex. 3.2–4)

Then one of the seraphs flew to me, holding a live coal that had been taken from the altar with a pair of tongs. The seraph touched my mouth with it and said: 'Now that this has touched your lips, your guilt has departed and your sin is blotted out.' Then I heard the voice of the Lord saying, 'Whom shall I send, and who will go for us?' And I said, 'Here am I; send me!' (Isa. 6.6–8)

The Hebrew word *hineni* occurs many times in the Hebrew Scriptures. It comes at moments of drama, moments of calling. Moses is drawn off the path by the sight of the bush that is burning but is not consumed; and he responds to this moment of mystery by saying, 'Here I am.' Isaiah, in a moment of crisis for the nation of Israel, after the death of King Uzziah, is given a vision of cherubim and seraphim in the Temple, and a burning coal touches his lips, and he responds to this extraordinary moment by saying, 'Here I am.' In that moment of encounter with the divine, both Moses and Isaiah are inspired to let go of their previous lives, of all that they have tried to be and to do, and to say yes to this experience that is beyond words and beyond imagining.

It's not always so dramatic. The boy Samuel, asleep in the Temple, is woken by a quiet voice calling him in the night. He pads down the corridor to his priest, Eli – *hineni*, here I am, he says – but Eli has not called him and tells him to go back to bed and listen again. When he hears the voice, Samuel says, 'Speak, for your servant is listening' (1 Sam. 3.10). Mary, when the Angel Gabriel visits her, is quite offhand; she ponders what his greeting might mean, and is sceptical when she's told she's to have a son: 'How can this be, since I am a virgin?' But despite her scepticism, she makes a decision: 'Let it be with me according to your word' (Luke 1.34, 38).

Each of them takes the decision to let go, to leave behind the certainties of their life and move into the queasily unknown. Moses, as a result, is forced into conflict with Pharoah, repeatedly demanding that Pharoah sets his people free and repeatedly being rebuffed despite plague after plague after plague. Isaiah becomes a prophet, ill-treated and unloved like most prophets.

HERE I AM!

Samuel too becomes a prophet, dedicated to God, speaking truth to power. Mary becomes the bearer of Christ, and a sword pierces her soul; she stands at the foot of the cross watching her son be executed. Rumi, the great mystic, leaves all his books and goes off to start a new life. Madeleine Debrél deserts her comfortable life to live in the slums of Paris. Fannie Lou Hamer, too:

> Fannie Lou Hamer (1917–1977) is a contemplative exemplar because of her spiritual focus and resolve. Her practices spoke to the depth of her contemplative spirit. In the face of catastrophic suffering, Hamer worked, loved, sang, and resisted the powers that be. She was jailed, beaten, and hunted by the enforcers of the social order after registering to vote ... Hamer was centered; she drew power from the example of her parents in their struggle to transcend the impossible situation of their lives ... Adherence to the spiritual disciplines of civil rights activism required that she love the crucifier, bless the torturer, embrace the jailer, and pray for his or her salvation. She did this and more.[79]

Fannie was shot at, assaulted and beaten many times by racists and police officers in the southern USA, and died of exhaustion. 'I am sick and tired of being sick and tired' is inscribed on her grave. Or, as the Archdeacon of Southwark said to me once, 'Nobody said it was going to be easy.'

The Latin word for prayer – *preces* – comes from the same root as the word precarious. The lives of many who have been deeply inspired by the Spirit were painful and ended in torture and martyrdom. It is a narrow way: and the ground is not solid and the path is not clear. That's perhaps why the journey has resonance for so many queer people, Black people, women – people who are outside the mainstream and understand what it means for the ground on which we stand to be unstable and unreliable, people who seek a grounding in something beyond themselves, a deeper community, a cosmic sense of connection.

> Christ is ... a very queer divinity who is not just a father, but also a mother, and in all cases a lover. Christ's humanity is

both man-ity and woman-ity, and much that is in between or neither.[80]

However difficult it is, though, the journey is worth the effort. That's one of the many paradoxes of Jesus' teaching:

> 'Come to me, all you that are weary and are carrying heavy burdens, and I will give you rest. Take my yoke upon you, and learn from me; for I am gentle and humble in heart, and you will find rest for your souls. For my yoke is easy, and my burden is light.' (Matt. 11.28–30)

Hineni. Here I am. The process of simply turning towards the divine makes it happen. Turning up, quietly, reliably, day after day, through the dry times and the fruitful times, the times described by St Ignatius as times of consolation and times of desolation – this is what opens the doors between the world that we know and the world we can never know. The dry times certainly come. I often find myself trudging through the foothills of spirituality, with very little sense of where I'm going or what I'm doing. But these times are offset by glimmers of inspiration, brief instants during my silent prayer when I find myself disorientated and part of the unboundaried cosmos, or momentary meetings spirit to spirit which remind me what the journey is all about.

Zen Buddhism has a saying: 'Chop wood and carry water.' Stick to the knitting. Every journey starts with a single step. Keep on turning up. Here I am. The river of life flows on, endlessly and infinitely, and all we have to do is have the courage to step into it.

That's why a Rule of Life is helpful. It provides a structure and a framework to help with the discipline of simply turning up. It's easy to be sidetracked, to reach for your phone. It's easy to become complacent and to imagine that you have discovered the truths that need discovering. It's also easy to give up, thinking that your efforts are being unrewarded, you're not really seeing any difference, and the challenges in your life are not in any way lightening. That's when the Rule becomes important, because it will keep you on the path, help you to continue to chop wood and carry water, and make sure that, even if it doesn't feel like it, the doors of perception remain open so that the Spirit can continue to do her work.

That's why, too, being part of a spiritual community is more than helpful; it's essential. We all need companions on the journey. It can be hard to find the right community, I know. Churches and mosques and temples and synagogues are not always places where seekers can flourish. But it's helpful to engage with ancient spiritual traditions. They have survived and changed through the wisdom and work of many people committed to the life-giving process of spiritual exploration.

For most people, the tradition in which they grew up is the best to explore; familiarity can help navigate the thickets, and childhood resonances are very strong. But you may have very few childhood resonances, or you may, perhaps because of rejection or trauma, need to find a new tradition – leaving Catholicism for Buddhism or Hinduism for Christianity. Keep searching. Even in these secular times, there are a remarkable number of communities committed to the open exploration of spirituality. Wisdom is universal.

This is from Chief Dan Evehema, quoted by Alice Walker in her book *We Are the Ones We Have Been Waiting For*:

> You have been telling the people that this is the Eleventh Hour. Now you must go back and tell the people that this IS the hour. And there are things to be considered ... Where are you living? What are you doing? What are your relationships? Are you in right relation? Where is your water? Know your garden. It is time to speak your truth, create your community, be good to each other. And do not look outside yourself for the leader. This could be a good time!
>
> There is a river flowing now very fast. It is so great and swift, that there are those who will be afraid. They will try to hold on to the shore. They will feel they are being torn apart and will suffer greatly. Know the river has its destination. The elders say we must let go of the shore – push off into the middle of the river, keep our eyes open, and our heads above the water. See who is in there with you and celebrate.

At this time in history, we are to take nothing personally, least of all, ourselves. For when we do, our spiritual growth and journey comes to a halt. The time of the lone wolf is over. Gather yourselves; Banish the word 'struggle' from your attitude and your vocabulary. All that we do now must be done in a sacred manner and in celebration. We are the ones we have been waiting for![81]

At the start of this book I said I was hoping to offer a distillation of what I have learnt over the past 40 years. Here is a final distillation into five words:

Love is the life force.

I am very sure that love is what brought the cosmos into being. Love is what gives life. It's the word I use to describe those infinitesimal bursts of energy and light that form the dynamic creative dance of everything that exists. Love is the light of life. Flickers of love refracted through crystal create a rainbow of promise that never fails to lift the heart. And, according to the first letter of John:

God is love, and those who live in love abide in God, and God abides in them. (1 John 4.16)

William Blake understood the task we are given at birth:

We are put on earth a little space,
that we may learn to bear the beams of love.[82]

Religion, spirituality, faith traditions – they clothe the bones of love with living, breathing, fragile flesh.

In these times of huge challenge, when the future seems frightening and the present full of conflict, it's even more important to find a tradition that works for you and burrow into it. Burrow into it, enjoying the bricolage of writings and prayers and music and art and stories. Burrow into it, knowing that it will bring together all that makes you fully alive: action, contemplation, justice, creativity, despair, hope. Knowing that the journey will be rewarding, albeit tough and demanding commitment. Burrow into it, knowing that it will take you into surprising spaces where what you thought was solid turns out to be ephemeral, and what you thought was ephemeral turns out to be the ground on which your soul can dance.

Burrow into it, knowing that underneath everything lies a unity too deep for words. At the heart of the dance, at the top of the mountain is a place beyond reason, beyond sight, beyond existence, where we are mysteriously brought into infinite oneness. Where every word ever spoken, every breath ever breathed, every hope ever hoped are melded into a love utterly beyond any love we can possibly imagine.

Draw the words of Psalm 46 into the depths of your spirit:

Be still, and know that I am God! (Ps. 46.10)

Acknowledgements

This book had its origins in the Exploring Spirit season at St John's, Waterloo, in spring 2024. So I'm grateful to Georgia Ashwell, Grey Collier, Martin Gainsborough, Annette Kaye, Chine MacDonald, Sharon Moughtin and Hasima Zaman for all their thoughtful reflections.

Thanks to all on the Encounter Course in spiritual direction, 2021–24, and to Julie Dunstan, my always wise and always challenging spiritual director.

Thanks to David Shervington, Christine Smith and the team at Canterbury Press for their support and guidance.

Thanks to the whole congregation of St John's for your joyful seriousness and enquiring commitment.

Above all, huge thanks to Shanon, my most supportive critic, who keeps my feet on the ground even when my head's in the clouds.

Further reading

Of the many thousands of books written on these topics, here are some that have inspired and/or informed me:

Armstrong, Karen, *Sacred Nature*, London: Vintage, 2023.
Carter, Richard, *The City is My Monastery*, Norwich: Canterbury Press, 2019.
Cassidy, Sheila, *Good Friday People*, London: Darton, Longman and Todd, 1991.
Critchley, Simon, *On Mysticism*, London: Profile Books, 2024.
Douglas, Kelly Brown, *The Black Christ*, New York: Orbis Books, 2019.
Ford, Mandy, *God, Gender, Sex and Nature*, London: Jessica Kingsley Publishers, 2019.
Gospels of Matthew, Mark, Luke and John, New Revised Standard Version or *The Message* translations.
Grigg, Ray, *The New Lao Tzu: A Contemporary Tao Te Ching*, Boston: Tuttle, 1995.
Harrington, Joel, *Dangerous Mystic: A Biography of Meister Eckhart*, London: Penguin, 2018.
Kermani, Navid, *Everyone, Wherever You Are, Come One Step Closer*, Cambridge: Polity Press, 2023.
Kimmerer, Robin Wall, *Braiding Sweetgrass*, London: Penguin, 2013.
Loach, Mikhaela, *It's Not That Radical: Climate Action to Transform Our World*, London: Dorling Kindersley, 2023.
Oliver, Mary, *Selected Poems*, Boston: Beacon Press, 2004.
Parke, Simon, *Conversations with Meister Eckhart*, Guildford: White Crow Books, 2009.
Riley, Cole Arthur, *This Here Flesh*, London: Hodder and Stoughton, 2024.
Rumi, *Selected Poems*, London: Penguin, 2024.
Safi, Omid, *Memories of Muhammad: Why the Prophet Matters*, New York: HarperOne, 2010.
Thurman, Howard, *Jesus and the Disinherited*, Boston: Beacon Press, 1976.
Walker, Alice, *We Are the Ones We Have Been Waiting For*, New York: The New Press, 2006.

References

1 Some names and identifying details have been changed to protect the privacy of individuals.
2 Transliteration of the biblical YHWH.
3 Pam McCarroll, Thomas St James O'Connor and Elizabeth Meakes, 2005, 'Assessing Plurality in Spirituality Definitions', in Augustine Meier, Thomas St James O'Connor and Peter L. VanKatwyk (eds), *Spirituality and Health: Multidisciplinary Explorations*, Wilfrid Laurier University Press, pp. 44–59.
4 Eamonn Duffy, 1994, *The Stripping of the Altars: Traditional Religion in England 1400–1580*, Yale University Press.
5 Jason Josephson-Storm, 2017, *The Myth of Disenchantment: Magic, Modernity, and the Birth of the Human Sciences*, University of Chicago Press, p. 3.
6 Charlie Bell, 2024, *Queer Redemption: How Queerness Changes Everything We Know about Christianity*, Darton, Longman and Todd, p. 58.
7 Charles Taylor, 2007, *A Secular Age*, Harvard University Press, p. 18.
8 George Herbert, 1975, 'Prayer (I)', in *The Metaphysical Poets*, ed. Helen Gardner, Penguin, p. 124.
9 Chinua Akebe, (1964, *The Role of the Writer in a New Nation*, New York: CBS.
10 https://cac.org/daily-meditations/the-spirit-in-jesus/, accessed 21.08.2025.
11 Percy Bysshe Shelley, 2002, 'Ozymandias', in Donald H. Reiman and Neil Fraistat (eds), *Shelley's Poetry and Prose*, W. W. Norton.
12 Mary Oliver, 1998, 'Have you ever tried to enter the long black branches', *West Wind: Poems and Prose Poems*, Mariner.
13 The number 42 is, in Douglas Adams, *The Hitchhiker's Guide to the Galaxy* (Pan Books, 2009), the 'Answer to the Ultimate Question of Life, the Universe, and Everything'.
14 Gerard Loughlin, 2007, *Queer Theology: Rethinking the Western Body*, Blackwell, p. 116.
15 Jerome, Letter, Section 7, quoted in Adrian Thatcher, 2023, *Vile Bodies*, SCM Press, p. 115.

16 Anguttara Nikaya (sutta 1, 21), quoted by Philip Moffat, 2007, *Awakening in the Body*, Shambala Sun.
17 John of the Cross, 1957, *Spiritual Canticle*, 17–18, trans. E. Allison Peers, Newman Press.
18 R. P. Lawson, 1957, *Origen, The Song of Songs: Commentary and Homilies*, Paulist Press, p. 44.
19 Isabelle Hamley, 2024, *Embracing Humanity: A Journey Towards Becoming Flesh*, BRF Ministries.
20 Mona Haydar, 2020, *Good Body*, https://www.youtube.com/watch?v=2SM39XoBVgw, accessed 21.07.2025.
21 Alexander von Humboldt, 1860, *Letters of Alexander von Humboldt to Varnhagen von Ense*, Rudd and Carleton, p. 194.
22 Tim Flinders, 2016, 'Divine Wilderness: John Muir's spiritual and political journey', *The Ecologist*, 6 May, https://theecologist.org/2016/may/06/divine-wilderness-john-muirs-spiritual-and-political-journey, accessed 21.07.2025.
23 Masnavi, III, 4300–4, https://sufism.org/origins/rumi/jewels/rumi-on-spirit-2, accessed 12.08.2025.
24 See Chief Dan George, 2017, *The Best of Chief Dan George*, Hancock House Publishers.
25 Biologist J. T. S. Haldane in response to a question by a group of theologians on what he had learnt about the Creator from the study of creation.
26 Pierre Teilhard de Chardin, 1969, *Hymn of the Universe*, Fount.
27 Gerard Manley Hopkins, 'Pied Beuty'.
28 Ian Phillips, 2025, 'Small Mammal Recovery and River Restoration on Hackney Marshes', https://www.youtube.com/watch?v=F8RzXC-3MWaM, accessed 21.07.2025.
29 Cole Arthur Riley, 2024, *This Here Flesh: Spirituality, Liberation, and the Stories that Make Us*, Hodder & Stoughton.
30 Rumi, *Masnavi*, 1, adapted from *The Masnavi*, trans. E. H. Whitfield, 2014, Create Space Independent Publishing Platform.
31 'Special Ecumenical Service of Lament', 2023, Friends of Sabeel North America, https://www.fosna.org/preach-palestine-blog/special-ecumenical-service-of-lament, accessed 22.07.2025.
32 Riley, *This Here Flesh*.
33 T. S. Eliot, 1969, 'Journey of the Magi', *Collected Poems 1909–1962*, Faber & Faber.
34 Riley, *This Here Flesh*, p. 168.
35 The Archbishops' Council, 2000, *Common Worship: Pastoral Services*, Church House Publishing, p. 269.
36 John Donne, 'Holy Sonnet 6', in Helen Gardener (ed.), 1975, *The Metaphysical Poets*, Penguin, p. 85.
37 *Common Worship: Pastoral Services*, p. 268.

REFERENCES

38 From the song 'Peace is Flowing Like a River', authorship unknown. See https://www.godsongs.net/2017/11/peace-is-flowing-like-river.html, accessed 12.08.2025.
39 David Cayley, 2005, *The Rivers North of the Future: The Testament of Ivan Illich*, House of Anansi Press, p. 227.
40 Cayley, *The Rivers North*, p. 31.
41 *The Bhagavad Gita*, trans. Juan Mascaro, 1962, Penguin Classics, Chapter 4:7–8, p. 61.
42 Samuel Munayer, at 'The First Christians were Palestinians', Bloomsbury Central Baptist Church, London, 23 December 2024.
43 Martin Luther King, 2010, *Where Do We Go from Here: Chaos or Community?*, Beacon Press.
44 Toni Morrison, 2016, *Beloved*, Vintage, referenced by Riley, *This Here Flesh*, p. 104.
45 Howard Thurman, *Jesus and the Disinherited*, Beacon Press, 1996.
46 Mikaela Loach, 2023, *It's Not That Radical: Climate Action to Transform Our World*, Dorling Kindersley, p. 189.
47 *Laudato Si'*, para. 217, https://www.vatican.va/content/francesco/en/encyclicals/documents/papa-francesco_20150524_enciclica-laudato-si.html, accessed 12.08.2025.
48 Quoted in Othman Llewellyn, Fazlun Khalid et al., 2024, *Al-Mizan: Covenant for the Earth*, The Islamic Foundation for Ecology and Environmental Sciences, Birmingham, UK, p. 12, See www.almizan.earth, accessed 21.08.2025.
49 The Last Sermon of the Prophet Muhammad, delivered on the Ninth Day of Dul-Hijjah 10AH (9 March 632 CE) and quoted in Akbar S. Ahmed, 1999, *What is Islam?*, Tauris, p. 21.
50 Rowan Williams, 2024, *Passions of the Soul*, Bloomsbury, p. 81.
51 Ted Falcon and David Blatner, 2019, *Judaism for Dummies*, 2nd edn, John Wiley, p. 42.
52 The Archbishops' Council, 2006, *Common Worship: Times and Seasons*, Church House Publishing, p. 334.
53 *Common Worship: Times and Seasons*, p. 335.
54 From 'The Exsultet', fifth to seventh century; author and translator unknown.
55 The Qur'an, Surah An-Noor 24.35, trans. M. A. S. Abdel Haleem, 2010, Oxford University Press.
56 Ṣaḥīḥ al-Bukhārī 6316, Ṣaḥīḥ Muslim 763, https://www.abuaminaelias.com/dailyhadithonline/2020/12/21/prophet-asks-nur-noor/, accessed 12.08.2025.
57 Gayatri mantra, https://thepunchmagazine.com/the-byword/poetry/world-poetry-prose-portfolio-tokya-tanka-and-other-poems, accessed 12.08.2025.

58 John of the Cross, 1990, *Dark Night of the Soul*, trans. E. Allison Peers, Image, p. 33.
59 Henry Vaughan, 'The Night', in Gardener (ed.), *The Metaphysical Poets*, p. 280.
60 Thomas Merton, Prayer before Midnight Mass, Christmas 1941, in Thomas Merton, 2001, *Dialogues with Silence: Prayers and Drawings*, ed. Jonathan Montaldo, HarperSanFrancisco, pp. xiii–xiv.
61 Simon Critchley, 2024, *On Mysticism: The Experience of Ecstasy*, Profile Books, p. 151.
62 Critchley, *On Mysticism*, p. 151.
63 Madeleine Delbrêl, 2024, *The Holiness of Ordinary People*, Ignatius Press.
64 Madeleine Delbrêl, 2000, *We The Ordinary People of the Streets*, Eerdmans, https://www.communio-icr.com/files/43.4_Delbrel_We_the_Ordinary.pdf, accessed 27.07.2025.
65 Riley, *This Here Flesh*.
66 Malidoma Patrice Somé, 1995, *Of Water and the Spirit: Ritual, Magic, and Initiation in the Life of an African Shaman*, Penguin.
67 Alejandro Nava, 2020, *Street Scriptures: Between God and Hip-Hop*, University of Chicago Press.
68 Meister Eckhart, 'Beati Pauperes Spiritu', Sermon on Matthew 5.3.
69 *The Cloud of Unknowing and the Book of Privy Counselling*, trans. William Johnston, 1973, Doubleday.
70 *The Cloud of Unknowing and the Book of Privy Counselling*, trans. William Johnston.
71 Si comprehendus, non est Deus. Augustin, Sermon 67 on the New Testament, para 5, https://www.newadvent.org/fathers/160367.htm, accessed 12.08.2025.
72 Pseudo Dionysus, 1980, *Mystical Theology*, 1.1, trans. C. E. Rolt, SPCK.
73 Sheikh Hafidh Sulaiman ibn al-Qunduzi Hanafi, cited in Yanabiul Mawaddah, Istanbul edition, p. 69.
74 Muhyiddin Ibn Al-Arabi, 1978, *The Tarjumān al-Ashwāk: A Collection of Mystical Odes*, trans. Reynold A. Nicholson, Theosophical Books, p. 19.
75 Qur'an, Surah Qaaf, v16, trans. M.A.L. Abdel Haleem, 2010, Oxford University Press (amended for inclusive language).
76 Riley, *This Here Flesh*.
77 Introduction, 1980, *The Bezels of Wisdom*, trans. R. W. J. Austin, Paulist Press, p. 23.
78 Irenaeus, *Adversus Haereses* (Against Heresies), book 4, chapter 20, paragraph 7, https://www.earlychristianwritings.com/text/irenaeus-book4.html (adapted), accessed 12.08.2025.

REFERENCES

79 Barbara A. Holmes, 2017, *Joy Unspeakable: Contemplative Practices of the Black Church*, 2nd edn, Fortress Press, pp. 125–6, 127.
80 Critchley, *On Mysticism*, p. 250.
81 Credited to Chief Dan Evehema, who passed on in 1999 aged 108, and quoted in Alice Walker, 2007, *We Are The Ones We Have Been Waiting For: Inner Light in a Time of Darkness*, Weidenfeld & Nicolson.
82 William Blake, 'The Little Black Boy', 2007, *Songs of Innocence and of Experience*, Penguin Classics.

www.ingramcontent.com/pod-product-compliance
Lightning Source LLC
LaVergne TN
LVHW041637060526
838200LV00040B/1608